# PAPER BULLETS

## A BRIEF STORY OF PSYCHOLOGICAL WARFARE IN WORLD WAR II

# PAPER BULLETS

## A BRIEF STORY OF PSYCHOLOGICAL WARFARE IN WORLD WAR II

LEO J. MARGOLIN

*Field representative of the Overseas Branch, United States Office of War Information, attached to the Psychological Warfare Branch, Allied Forces Headquarters, as news editor, 1943-1945.*

**COACHWHIP PUBLICATIONS**
Greenville, Ohio

Dedicated to the men and women of the Overseas Branch, United States Office of War Information, who were called from the offices of America's newspapers, news services, magazines, movie studios, radio stations, advertising agencies, print shops, book publishers, publicity firms and universities to serve their country as propagandists in time of war, and who discharged their duties, frequently under enemy fire and bombings, loyally, courageously and expertly.

L. J. M.



*Paper Bullets* published 1946
Leo J. Margolin (1910-1971)


CoachwhipBooks.com

ISBN 1-61646-492-5
ISBN-13 978-1-61646-492-9

# I
# MEET PSYCHOLOGICAL WARFARE

Psychological warfare is a fancy word for propaganda. Both mean the same thing: use of words and ideas as a weapon of warfare against the enemy.

Until we got into the shooting phase of World War II, we had held the short end of the straw in world psychological warfare, principally because Americans are as allergic to the word "propaganda" as is a fish to a pile of dry sand. We were raised on cold milk, ice cream sodas and baseball. Propaganda was never consciously part of our diet.

To Americans, propaganda has always meant a horrible, nasty word like "spit." It always had a foreign meaning and we considered it good only for foreigners. Yet we Americans have been exposed to propaganda under a different name in our everyday life. We call it advertising.

Propaganda, or advertising, or psychological warfare, has been one of the most effective weapons of this war on our side. Directly and indirectly it has saved thousands of American and Allied lives. At the same time, propaganda almost defeated us before we hit back.

HEUTE LEBST DU NOCH. Du kämpfst mit unzureichenden Waffen, mit mangelhafter Ausrüstung, von halbgeschulten Einheiten umgeben. Aber — Du lebst. Tausende Deiner Kameraden, viele Deiner eigenen Freunde sind gefallen. Es war schlimm, aber Du bist noch entkommen. Du lebst. Deine Offiziere verwerfen Deine Gedanken, dass das nur eine Kampfpause ist. Es besteht Hoffnung, denn — Du lebst.

MORGEN KANN ES LOSGEHEN, wie es auf einmal losging am Atlantikwall, bei Avranches und St. Lo. Morgen: Plötzliches, pausenloses Trommelfeuer aller Kaliber, rollender Einsatz von Jabos; tausende von Fliegenden Festungen; Bombenteppiche; Panzer, panzerbrechende Raketenwaffen und die neuen Flammenwerfer. Alles, was Du bisher gesehen hast, war im Vergleich damit ein Kinderspiel. Morgen: die Hölle.

ÜBERMORGEN WIRD ES AUS SEIN, und Du bist entweder tot, ein Krüppel oder Kriegsgefangener. Die Entscheidung darüber liegt vielleicht an Dir selbst. Deshalb bedenke jetzt, was Du machen wirst, wenn Du noch am Leben bist, wenn die Materialschlacht über Dich hinwegrollt. Dann ist vielleicht für Dich Gelegenheit, Dein Leben zu retten. Viele werden sich ergeben müssen. So mancher wird aber sterben müssen, weil er die Wahl zu spät getroffen hat.

## WELCHE WAHL TRIFFST DU?

ZG 82

The mere fact that Germans did surrender with this leaflet does not mean that they will surrender in the future to the idea that they lost. The loss of the war does not occur to them except as a temporary inconvenience. "When all hell breaks loose" could very well apply to the American peope when they discover that the Germans will have really won the war by winning the psychological war.

TODAY YOU ARE STILL ALIVE. You fight with insufficient weapons, poorly equipped, surrounded by half-trained units. But—you are alive. Thousands of your comrades, many of your own friends, have died. It was bad, but so far you have escaped. You are alive. Your officers dismiss your thought that this is only a lull. There is hope, for—you are alive.

TOMORROW ALL HELL MAY BREAK LOOSE—just as it started up all of a sudden at the Atlantic Wall, near Avranches and St. Lo. Tomorrow: sudden uninterrupted barrages from guns of all calibres, continuous dive-bombing, thousands of Flying Fortresses and carpets of bombs; tanks, anti-tank rockets, and the new flame throwers. Everything you have seen so far was child's play compared with that. Tomorrow: Hell.

DAY AFTER TOMORROW IT WILL BE OVER and you will be either dead, a cripple, or a prisoner of war. The decision about that is perhaps in your own hands. Consider, therefore, what you will do if you are still alive when the Materialschlacht (battle of material) has rolled over you. Then there may be an opportunity for you to save your life. Many will be forced to surrender. Many another will die, however, because he made his choice too late.

**WHAT IS YOUR CHOICE ?**

A NOTE ABOUT THE LEAFLET: Written especially for an Army Group, to be used on their signal and targets specified by them only.

Although advertising generally is not connected with propaganda, advertising is nothing more than a respectable name and form for propaganda. Selling an idea to chew only a certain brand of gum, or drive only a certain make of car, is propaganda, not too far removed from selling an enemy soldier or people the idea of surrender because their cause is hopeless.

Because advertising is decorated in four beautiful colors and comes on slick paper with slick-sounding words, doesn't purge it of what it is: propaganda to sell you a product or an idea.

A perfect example of the potency of advertising as propaganda is the phenomenal success of the electric refrigerator called "Frigidaire." So effective has been Frigidaire's advertising that nine out of ten people owning a mechanical refrigerator will refer to their refrigerating unit as a "Frigidaire," although it may be an Electrolux, which runs by gas; a Philco, a GE, a Hotpoint, or a Cold Spot. Frigidaire's advertising geniuses have adroitly, although indirectly, sold the consumer public the idea that an electric refrigerator can be only a "Frigidaire."

And via the same propaganda route we refer to chilled gelatin dessert as "Jello," which is a smartly advertised trade name, and in discussing slide fasteners we invariably call them "Zippers" although that too is an advertised brand name.

A good test of the effectiveness of propaganda as reflected in advertising is to ask any American what products he connects with the slogans "The Pause That Refreshes," "99 and 44/100 per cent pure," and "Not a Cough in a Carload." You would think there was something wrong with anyone who couldn't give you the answers "Coca Cola," "Ivory Soap" and "Old Gold Cigarettes" in quick succession.

Because we failed to connect propaganda with advertising, we made our first mistake in World War II by either ignoring it or brushing it off as good only for use by the British, the French or the Russians. Sometime after the shooting started we caught on fast because Americans, when they must, get very realistic and very mad.

It never occurred even to advertising-conscious Americans that pieces of paper imprinted with ideas in words and pictures could be used for anything except selling refrigerators, Coca Cola, chewing gum or for making spitballs.

We know now—with the spared lives of thousands of American soldiers as indisputable proof—that these same words, properly put together and delivered to the right people at the right time, have helped us immeasurably to win the military part of the global war.

The war of words and ideas as part of total war—and not as a weapon of warfare exclusively—remains to be won. Like advertising all psychological warfare is cumulative. And like mustard gas, which clings to the ground for months after battle, psychological warfare and its poison of hate and distrust linger on for years.

Today, that poison, spread by words and ideas, hangs like so much mustard gas not only over Germany and Japan from whence it emanated, but over the entire world. The poison is ready at all times and is sufficiently potent to destroy the unwary.

The best defense against this weapon is a complete knowledge of what it is, how it works, what are its objectives, and what and where have been its successes.

# II
# PSYCHOLOGICAL WARFARE IN HISTORY

Psychological warfare is not a German invention. All the Germans did was to improve its technique.

From its origin, as an ancient weapon, psychological warfare has weathered the ages so well that today, atomic bomb or no, it remains one of the most deadly weapons of modern warfare.

The pattern—employed 2,500 years ago by Xerxes, the Persian General, who decided on rumor-mongering for his psychological warfare—was used successfully by the Germans in building up the myth of their military invincibility.

Xerxes scared the daylights out of Greek warriors by spreading the story that when the Persians shot off their arrows they shut out the light of the sun. The Germans scared Europe out of its wits, conquering Austria and Czechoslovakia without firing more than a stray shot here and there.

When Hannibal tried rumor-mongering as his weapon of psychological warfare, his success was phenomenal. He sent rumors of "a secret weapon" over the Pyrenees, the Alps and the Appenines to his Roman enemies. His rumor mongers carefully spread the story of the "secret weapon," adding in sinister whispers: "It is powerful; it cannot be stopped!" And just to make the mental devastation complete the rumor spreaders added: "What's more, it cannot be pierced!"

It didn't require too much mental mulling by the Romans to say what millions of moderns said of the Germans more than 2,000 years later, "How can we resist?"

For the Romans, the moment they asked themselves that question, it was the end of the battle before it started. Hannibal's rumors had turned a perfectly good army into fright and then into panic. Instead of fighting, the Roman legions milled about like frightened children.

That's how Hannibal won the Battle of Trebia more than 200 years before Christ. The Romans discovered too late that the "secret weapon" was a herd of armored elephants.

A not unimportant aspect of psychological warfare is the weapon of scapegoatism, a device as old as history itself. The Germans borrowed heavily from history in developing their scapegoat technique as a method of taking the blame of gross bestiality away from themselves and as a convenient means of concealing their real motives in their plan for world conquest.

One of history's most famous fiddlers, although certainly one of the least proficient, Emperor Nero, was suspected in 64 A.D. of having set the great fire of Rome himself. There is no proof of his guilt, but the scandalous Nero did fix the blame upon the Christians, as a convenient scapegoat, torturing and executing them to turn suspicion from himself.

That was not very different from the crimes of Adolf Hitler and the German people, who made Nero and others like him appear as two-penny pikers. The German people, with Hitler and his stooges as the spark-plug, murdered 6,000,000 Jews in Europe to achieve only one phase of their scapegoat campaign.

The blame belongs principally with the Germans. The remaining guilt should be on the consciences of the people of the world, who though horror-stricken, failed to raise their voices in effective protest. The cumulative total of German psychological warfare in this instance was so overwhelming that hundreds of thousands of people believed the mad-dog mouthings of the Nazis. Now, in retrospect, we are certain that the Germans are not entirely to blame. J. Howard McGrath, Solicitor General of the United States, speaking recently in New York, stated:

"We sat by while six million persons of one creed were slain in the gas chambers of Germany, and did not raise our voices in much protest because it was happening to the Jews of Europe. It was far away.

"We almost gave encouragement to the Nazis by our silent acquiescence. We almost said that it was all right to take the life of a human being as long as it was the life of a Jew."

History provided many precedents from which the Germans could borrow. It meant turning the clock back, but what did that mean to the Nazis. During the reign of Trajan, merely being a Christian was a criminal offense, as indicated in Trajan's letters to Pliny in 112 A.D. The Romans devoted a large part of their time in persecuting and scapegoating Christians.

An important historical precedent occurred between 1348 and 1350, during the Hundred Years' War, when the Black Death—a devasting outbreak of bubonic plague—swept over Europe. More than 25,000,000 people, probably one-quarter of the population of Europe, died. We know now this disease is spread by rats and fleas. The total ignorance of sanitation in fourteenth century Europe was the prime cause of the epidemic. But rumor quickly fastened the responsibility on the Jews, charging that they brought on the scourge by poisoning the wells. Because of their observance of the ancient Mosaic dietary laws, the Jews suffered relatively less from the plague than their neighbors. But this very fact intensified their victimization. They were depicted as in league with the devil to save themselves and spread the disease to Christians. Massacres of Jews took place in France, Spain, Italy, Switzerland, Germany, and other plague-ridden countries.

The Nazis in their persecution of the Jews made it a crusade. Their propaganda was clever because it successfully beclouded their real motive. While the Germans made it appear that their anti-Semitic campaign was strictly a movement against the Jews, actually it was a smokescreen, hiding their military preparations. Coincidentally, the campaign quietly served their purpose of developing anti-Semitism into a military weapon for later use.

It. was a deadly campaign because most of the world was in complete ignorance of what the Nazis were *really* doing.

In the German economic crises of the 1870s, Heinrich von Treischke revived the latent anti-Jewish feeling in Germany by coining the slogan. "The Jews are our misfortune," which was later adopted by Julius Streicher, the insane Nazi Jew-baiter in his obscene publication, *Der Stuermer.*

Hitler discovered anti-Semitism was a shrewd device for gaining power. Herman Rauschnig quotes Hitler in *The Voice of Destruction,* as telling his cronies:

"My Jews are a valuable hostage given to me by the democracies. Anti-Semitic propaganda in all countries is an indispensable medium for the extension of our political campaign. You will see how little time we shall need in order to upset the ideas . . . of all the world, simply and purely by attacking Judaism."

* * * *

Even the blood-curdling shrieks of American Indians were weapons of psychological warfare. It was designed to terrorize their enemies, thus reducing their will to fight or even to resist. The Germans improved on that technique in the early days of World War II. Their famous screamer planes, which emitted nerve-shattering shrieks, were nothing more than a weapon to frighten. The scream of sirens attached to Nazi planes did not make the bombing any more or less terrible, but it did take a toll on the nerves of both the French Army and the civilians, accelerating their desire to call the war quits.

Some of our ingenious American fliers devised their own version of this type of warfare on the North African front. A Mitchell bomber crew, which had been bombing Italian rail communications carried a couple of bundles of leaflets and some wine bottles every time they went out to bomb. Questioned by a

# Wo ist Hitler?

? ? ? ? ? ? ? ? ? ? ? ? ?

■ **Wann hat Hitler sich zuletzt öffentlich gezeigt ?**

Am 30. Juni, bei der Beerdigung General Dietls.

■ **Wann wurde Hitlers Stimme zuletzt gehört?**

Kurz nach dem Attentat vom 20. Juli. Damals versicherte der Führer, dass er unter dem Schutz der Vorsehung stehe und sich der allerbesten Gesundheit erfreue. Seither ist viel geschehen. Frankreich, Belgien und Griechenland wurden befreit.

■ **Der Führer hatte nichts dazu zu bemerken.**

Die Deutschen mussten fast das ganze Gebiet von Jugoslawien räumen und verloren grosse Teile von Holland Ungarn, der Tschechoslowakei und den Baltischen Staaten.

■ **Immer noch kein Wort von Adolf Hitler.**

Sein berühmtester General, Generalfeldmarschall Rommel, wurde zu Grabe getragen.

■ **Der Führer fiel durch Abwesenheit auf.**

Hitlers frühere Bundesgenossen, Rumänien und Bulgarien, erklärten Deutschland den Krieg; Finnland schloss Frieden.

■ **Der grosse Redner blieb stumm.**

Er überliess es Himmler, das « Volkssturm »-Ge-

**A good example of what Marshall Von Hindenburg was talking about is this leaflet of the strategic variety thrown at German soldiers on the Italian front. Its purpose is to create distrust in the German soldier's mind for Hitler as a military and political leader and to fan the flames of resentment, revolt and perhaps surrender in the enemy's soldier's heart.**

setz zu erlassen - obwohl gerade bei dieser Gelegenheit eine persönliche, direkte Aeusserung vom Führer angebracht, ja notwendig gewesen wäre.

■ **Statt eines zündenden Aufrufs gab es indessen nur ein paar trockene Bemerkungen, die angeblich von Hitler stammten, aber von einer fremden Stimme am deutschen Rundfunk verlesen wurden.**

Im Westen und im Osten überschritten die Alliierten die Grenzen des Reiches; Aachen, die Kaiserstadt, wurde von den Amerikanern genommen.

■ **Hitlers Schweigen hielt an.**

Dann wurde das öffentliche Auftreten des Führers als besondere Attraktion für den 8. November angekündigt. Wie in jedem Jahr sollte Hitler das Andenken an den missglückten Bierkeller-Putsch von 1923 rednerisch begehen. Im letzten Augenblick wurde die Gedächtnisfeier überraschend abgesagt — und als sie dann ein paar Tage später ebenso überraschend wieder angesetzt wurde, da war es keineswegs Hitler, dessen Stimme die Nation vernahm, sondern wiederum und noch einmal — Heinrich Himmler!

■ **Durch Himmlers Mund liess Hitler den Deutschen mitteilen, dass er zu sehr beschäftigt sei, um von seinem Hauptquartier aus ein paar Worte ins Mikrophon zu sprechen...**

Der Landser, der für Hitler sterben soll, muss sich fragen:

# Wo ist Hitler?
# Warum spricht Hitler nicht?

T/29

*(Translation)*

# Where is Hitler?

? ? ? ? ? ? ? ? ? ? ? ?

■ **When was Hitler last seen in public?**

On June 30th, on the occasion of Generale Dietl's funeral.

■ **When was Hitler's voice last heard in public?**

Shortly after the attempt on his life, on July 20th. The Führer assured his listeners that he was under the special protection of Providence, and that his health was excellent. Since then much has happened.

France, Belgium and Greece were liberated.

■ **The Führer had nothing to say.**

The Germans had to evacuate most of Yugoslavia and lost important parts of Holland, Hungary, Czechoslovakia and the Baltic States.

■ **Still no word from Adolf Hitler.**

His most famous general, Field Marshal Rommel, was given a state funeral.

■ **The Führer was conspicuous by his absence.**

Hitler's former allies, Rumania and Bulgaria, declared war on Germany. Finland made peace.

■ **The great orator remained silent.**

He left it to Himmler to announce the establishment of the « Volkssturm. » At that time a direct, personal statement from the Führer would have been appropriate, indeed necessary.

■ **Instead of a stirring appeal, however, there were only a few dry remarks, allegedly by Hitler, but read by another voice over the German radio.**

In the West and in the East, the Allies entered the Reich territory; Aachen, the City of the Emperors, was taken by the Americans.

■ **Hitler' s silence continued.**

Then, as a special attraction, his public appearance was promised for November 8th. As in all previous years, the Führer was expected to celebrate with oratory the anniversary of the unsuccessful beer-cellar revolt of 1923. But at the very last moment the celebration was unexpectedly cancelled. And when, even more unexpectedly, it was scheduled again, the voice that was heard by the nation was not Hitler' s, no, but — once again — Heinrich Himmler' s.

■ **Through Himmler's mouth, Hitler informed the Germans that he was too busy to speak a few words into the microphone at his Headquarters...**

The German soldier, who is supposed to die for Hitler, must ask himself:

**Where is Hitler?**
**Why doesn't Hitler speak?**

**T/29**

psychological warfare officer, who failed to find this particular plane on his schedule, one member of the crew replied: "This is psychological warfare, Mac. Before we hit the target we take a fake bomb run over the nearest flak crew and throw these bottles and the leaflets out. They whistle just like bombs and the flak crew takes cover. Then we go on and bomb as per schedule."

That is a takeoff on "the strategy of terror," so cleverly improved by the Germans from the terror tactics of the ancient Japanese, and the African and South Sea Island tribes, who used the horrifying shrieks and war masks to frighten their enemies. And in principle it is no different from the terror inspired in advance of the armies of Philip of Macedonia and of Attila the Hun.

Each successive war has seen new improvements in psychological warfare techniques. Word and idea warfare was used extensively by the Allies in World War I and with devastating success. This unhappy state of affairs, for the Germans, prompted Marshal von Hindenburg to make a desperate appeal to the German Army and civilians. He said:

"The enemy conducts his campaign against our spirit by various means. He bombards our front, not only with a drumfire of artillery, but also with a drumfire of printed paper. Besides bombs, which kill the body, his airmen throw down leaflets which are intended to kill the soul.

"The enemy hopes that many a field-grey soldier will send home the leaflet which has innocently fluttered down from the air. At home it will pass from hand to hand and be discussed at the beer table, in families, in the drawing-room, in factories and in the street. Unsuspectingly many thousands consume the poison."

Marshal von Hindenburg was one German who, for once, was telling the truth.

☆ Vie Illustrée de

**FRANKLIN D. ROOSEVELT**

***32eme Président des États-Unis d'Amérique***

"Illustrated Life of Franklin D. Roosevelt" was distributed by the hundreds of thousands to give courage to the French and to keep alive the spark of resistance until tangible help could be sent. FDR was one of the best psychological warfare weapons on the Allied side. Mere mention of his name to French Maquis was enough to cause the blowing up of German ammunition dumps in occupied France, destruction of German supply roads and the killing of German soldiers.

## III
## PSYCHOLOGICAL WARFARE TYPES

Americans cannot pride themselves on their immunity or invincibility in the war of propaganda. Americans bit deeply into the enemy bait. For a time we swallowed the hook and were making substantial progress on the line toward the sinker.

Mentally we have always been receptive to propaganda because a large part of our diet has consisted of newspaper, magazine, billboard and radio advertising. The mere fact that the shooting war is now over does not mean that we are not swallowing enemy-manufactured propaganda. Although the enemy is defeated militarily, he is playing doggo with his propaganda.

As a defense of what is to come during "peace," it would be a good idea to paste into our hats for future reference this bit of intelligence distributed by the U.S. Office of War Information:

"Our enemies have an idea of war very different from ours.

"To them peace is not a normal state of affairs of a nation; war is not a painful and undesirable interruption of peace. To them, 'shooting war' is the continuation of permanent aggression in another form;

to them, war and peace differ only in calling for use of somewhat different weapons in a permanent war to advance aggressively their ideas of national interest.

"During a war, they add military aggression to the weapons they already have been using in time of 'peace'—informational and propaganda aggression, economic aggression and political aggression.

"The idea of total war is a part of the larger idea of permanent war. Since Nazi Germany and militarist Japan are always at war, the only difference between so-called peace and so-called war is the addition of real bullets to the bullets of propaganda, political and economic combinations.

"In time of peace, a very large number of Germans and Japanese work indirectly for victory; in time of war, everybody and everything work directly for victory."

All psychological warfare, whether carried on in "peace" or in war, has general objectives which can be classified as follows:

1. To weaken and gradually destroy the morale of the enemy and his will to resist.
2. To encourage and strengthen the spirit of resistance of friendly elements in territories overrun by the enemy.
3. To promote distrust of the enemy government and army on his home front and among neutrals.
4. To keep neutrals neutral, promote their friendship and sympathy and, if possible, procure their active co-operation.

From Eric Banse, one of Germany's outstanding experts in the field of psychological warfare, came this vivid explanation in 1931, when he wrote:

"Applied psychology as a weapon of war means propaganda intended to influence the attitude of nations at war. It is essential to attack the enemy nation in its weak spots—and what nation has not its weak spots—to undermine and break down its resistance, and to convince it that it is being deceived, misled and brought to destruction by its own government."

After reading this statement it is easy to understand why the Germans saturated our troops on the American Fifth Army front with leaflets based on an anti-Semitic theme.

The types of propaganda employed to achieve the objectives of psychological warfare can be divided into these classes:

1. Strategic propaganda: directed against the home populations of enemy countries with long-range radio as the principal vehicle, such as the Office of War Information's "Voice of America." Strategic leaflets, generally dropped by long-range heavy bombers, play an important, but lesser role.
2. Tactical propaganda: directed principally against enemy troops in the field. This was done most often by leaflets (or "paper bullets") fired by a special type artillery shell or dropped by tactical aircraft. Supplementing the leaflets at the front were short-range, usually

# GEGENANGRIFF

## Tatsachenbericht über Erlebnisse deutscher Soldaten

**Sturmmann Dietrich ████, SS-Div. Götz von Berlichingen:**

„Wir waren ein Stosstrupp bei Maringen, waren anscheinend zu weit vorgegangen, denn plötzlich erhielten wir nicht nur Granatwerferfeuer, sondern unsere eigene Art fetzte auch noch hinein. Wir nahmen Zuflucht in einem Keller. Auf einmal waren Panzer vor der Türe, warfen Handgranaten herein, und wir mussten uns ergeben. Behandlung ist soweit durchaus anständig."

**Unteroffizier Hans ████. 559. I.D.:**

„Wir sollten bei Nancy den Gegenangriff vortragen, bekamen aber Feuer noch als wir auf der Strasse waren und dann noch Jabos, die schossen aus allen Knopflöchern. Wir blieben ein paar Stunden liegen. Die ██ Kp. war zusammengeschossen, teils tot, teils verwundet. Unser Chef war schwer verwundet. Der Feldwebel stimmte ab, was wir machen sollten. Einer von uns konnte Englisch, der hat zu den Amerikanern hinübergerufen, wir haben unsere Waffen niedergelegt und sind geschlossen in die Gefangenschaft marschiert. 2 amerikanische Sanitäter haben den Chef sofort verbunden."

**Gefreiter Kurt ████ 113. Pz.-Brigade:**

„Mit Unterstützung von 200 Panzern griffen wir erfolgreich an. Bekamen heftiges Sperrfeuer und mussten nach links ausweichen und uns eingraben. Am nächsten Morgen griff der Amerikaner zum Gegenstoss an. Bekamen schweres Trommelfeuer—die Ausfälle waren sehr gross. Als dann die USA-Panzer kamen, da sagten die anderen Kameraden schon, es hätte keinen Sinn mehr. Wir ergaben uns der nachfolgenden Infanterie. Die Übermacht war einfach zu gross."

**Obergefreiter Ernst ████, 553. I.D.:**

„Der Amerikaner hatte Höhe 360 genommen. Wir bekamen Befehl zum Gegenangriff. Wir räumten auch die Höhe, aber oben im Wald blieb der Gegenangriff stecken. Wir brachten die Nacht im Wald zu. Früh morgens muss dann der Amerikaner seinerseits einen Gegenangriff gemacht haben, denn plötzlich waren seine Panzer hinter uns. Ich versuchte mit 3 anderen Kameraden feindeinwärts auszuweichen. Konnten aber nicht mehr zurück. Da mussten wir uns eben ergeben."

**Jeder Gegenangriff bedeutet: Nackte Menschenhände gegen Stahl. Jeder Gegenangriff bedeutet mehr sinnlose Opfer—aber: Jeder Gegenangriff bedeutet auch die Möglichkeit der Kriegsgefangenschaft.**

ZG 77

Here is psychological warfare of the tactical type and out of the mouths of the enemy. It uses the psychology of surrender even to the point of giving the German soldier a "five minute course in English," with heavy emphasis on surrender. This one caught a lot of grey-green flies.

TRANSLATION OF ZG 77 K

# COUNTER-ATTACK

## A factual report on experiences of German soldiers

**Sturmmann Dietrich ██████, SS Div. Götz von Berlichingen :**

"We were a combat patrol near Maringen, and apparently we went too far forward, for suddenly we received not only mortar fire but our own artillery went to work on us. We took refuge in a cellar. Suddenly, tanks were in front of the door, hand grenades were thrown in, and we had to give up. So far, the treatment is perfectly all right."

**Unteroffizier Hans ██████, 559. Inf. Div. :**

"We were to mount the counterattack near Nancy, but we were taken under fire while still on the approach road, and then fighter bombers appeared too and gave us a tough going over. We had to lie on the ground for several hours. ■ Company was shot up completely, they were nearly all dead or wounded. Our C.O. was gravely wounded. The top kick took a vote on what we should do. One of us knew English, and he yelled over to the Americans, we took off our arms and marched into captivity as a body. Two American First Aid Men immediately dressed the wounds of our C.O."

**Gefreiter Kurt ██████, 113. Pz.-Brigade :**

"We attacked successfully, supported by 200 tanks. We got heavy interdictory fire and had to move to the left and dig in. Next morning, the Americans counterattacked in their turn. We got a heavy barrage, and casualties ran high. Then, when the American tanks came, the other comrades already said there was no hope for us. We surrendered to the infantry which came up after them. The enemy's superiority was just too big."

**Obergefreiter Ernst ██████, 553. Inf. Div. :**

"The Americans had taken Hill 360. We received orders to counterattack. We cleared the hill, but up in the woods our counterattack bogged down. We spent the night in the woods. Early in the morning then the Americans must have made a counterattack of their own, for suddenly their tanks were behind us. I tried with three other comrades to go around them on the enemy side, but we counldn't get back. So we just had to surrender."

***Every counterattack means : Bare hands against steel. Every counterattack means more senseless sacrifices — But : Every counterattack means also the possibility of being taken prisoner.***

mobile, radio broadcasting stations, sound trucks and "walkie-talkie" sets, known among soldiers as "hog-calling."

3. Occupational propaganda (or education): carried on in territory that has been wrested from the enemy. The vehicles here are newspapers, radio, movies, public addresses, magazines, exhibits, etc. The objective in this type of propaganda is to develop a new outlook in people who have long been exposed to the poison of the enemy.

Not classed as a type, but important nevertheless, was propaganda directed to both friendly and unfriendly elements of populations who were not enemies, but who lived in territory occupied by the enemy.

Northern Italy is an excellent case in point. The majority of Italians there were on our side. It was necessary to sustain their morale and give them courage to continue their mental and physical resistance. At the same time the Fascists had to be subdued. The latter were frightened sufficiently by our flat statements of the retribution which would befall them when they fell into Allied hands.

One devastating result achieved with this type of psychological warfare was the complete smashing of an Italian spy training school operated by the Germans near Rome. Information of the school's existence reached Allied intelligence officers and within a few hours, Allied confetti soldiers began operating.

Leaflets were dropped on enemy-held Rome giving details which showed that the Allies knew all about this spy school. Listed in the leaflets were the names of all Italians involved. For additional emphasis, pictures of their colleagues, who had been captured and executed by the Allies were put into some of the leaflets. After the Americans had captured Rome, they found that these leaflets had caused such panic among the school's spy trainees, that virtually all the "students" had disappeared and had hidden themselves from the Germans.

No less an authority on the subject of propaganda than Adolph Hitler carefully set down its role in his "Mein Kampf," stating:

"The place of the artillery barrage as preparation for an infantry attack will in the future be taken by Revolutionary Propaganda. Its task is to break up the enemy psychologically before the armies begin to operate at all."

Since modern warfare does not begin with the shooting, leaving that formality as the final phase, there are certain steps which nations such as Germany and Japan take to carry out their long-planned aggressions.

First, there is the economic pressure which involves interference with a nation's access to sources of material, markets, capital and labor power. Germany's I. G. Farben Industrie, the huge chemical trust with world-wide agreements, is a good example of how economic warfare can be waged through secret cartels and preclusion agreements. America's synthetic rubber experiments were badly hampered because I. G. Farben chemists, on direct orders from Hitler, gave no information to American chemists although an exchange arrangement existed.

No. 1

# Five Minutes of English

**Blitz-Course**
**For German G. I.'s**

| GERMAN | ENGLISH | SIMPLIFIED PRONUNCIATION |
|---|---|---|
| Ich bin verwundet (krank). | I am wounded (sick). | *Ai em wuhnded (ssick).* |
| Wir ergeben uns. | We surrender. | *Ui ssörrenda.* |
| Danke für die Zigaretten. | Thanks for the cigarettes. | *Senks for se ssiggarets.* |
| Ich bin hungrig (durstig). | I am hungry (thirsty). | *Ai em hangri (sörsti).* |
| Bitte noch eine Tasse Kaffee. | Some more coffee, please. | *Sam mor koffi, plies.* |
| Wann kann ich mal baden ? | When can I take a bath ? | *Wen ken ai tek a bahs ?* |
| Wo ist warmes Wasser ? | Where is there hot water ? | *Wer is ser hot wota ?* |
| Ich möchte noch eine Decke. | I'd like another blanket. | *Aid laik anosa blänket.* |
| Gibt es was zu lesen ? | Got anything to read ? | *Gat änising tu ried ?* |
| Bitte um Schreibpapier. | A letter blank, please. | *E letta blenk, plies.* |
| Wann geht die Post ab ? | When does the mail leave ? | *When das se mehl liew ?* |

***A NOTE ABOUT THIS LEAFLET:*** **Chiefly for comparatively stationary but active situation as prevailed in early October. This is in line with the finding that the majority of German soldiers know why they should give up, but lack the opportunity. German counterattacks are such opportunities. ZG 74 K showed others.**

We are now in the process of breaking up the billion-dollar I. G. Farben Industrie to dissolve Germany's war-making ability.

The second step in waging warfare before the shooting begins is the use of propaganda, or the direct use of suggestion. This is carried on concurrently with the first step, economic warfare.

The third and final step is the use of military power while continuing the economic and propaganda warfare.

Psychological warfare without military warfare as the final and deciding phase is as useless as a pair of waterwings substituting for a submarine. No exponent of psychological warfare would pretend that it is a substitute for an atom bomb. It is strictly an auxiliary weapon which can produce fantastically successful results when applied under the right conditions.

The mass surrenders in Tunisia in May, 1943, which shortened the North Africa Campaign by a full thirty days, came only after Allied air and ground forces had given the Germans and the Italians a merciless pounding. Allied surrender leaflets did the rest.

A psychological warfare operative explained it this way to a division commander: "You see, General, it works something like this: you and your men push the krauts to the edge of the precipice and then we come along and push them over."

# NOTIZIE NAZIONI UNITE

Informazioni raccolte dal Servizio "Notizie Nazioni Unite", comprendenti notizie dalle Agenzie Alleate. Coloro che le utilizzeranno dovranno citare la fonte indicata nella notizia. La vendita di questo bollettino è assolutamente vietata.

Servizio "Notizie Nazioni Unite" Psychological Warfare Branch, AFHQ, Unit 12, APO 512 (Posta Militare Alleata)

N. 93 — 25 Novembre 1944

## SOMMARIO

### FRONTI DI GUERRA

Comunicato del fronte occidentale.
Un sommergibile britannico affonda due mercantili tedeschi.
Un « Heinkel » che lanciava siluri volanti abbattuto.
Entusiasmo in Francia per la liberazione di Strasburgo.
Comunicato del fronte italiano.
Il contributo italiano agli eserciti alleati.
Comunicato del fronte sovietico.
Comunicato del Maresciallo Tito.
Migliaia di chilogrammi di esplosivo disseminati dai tedeschi in Belgrado.
Comunicati e particolari sulle operazioni del fronte del Pacifico ed Estremo Oriente.
Particolari sul bombardamento di Tokio.
Gravi perdite inflitte ai tedeschi dai patrioti di Bologna.

### ITALIA LIBERATA

Una intervista dell'Ambasciatore d'Italia conte Carandini.
La sfilata per Roma di uno scaglione delle nuove unità di combattimento italiane.
Le norme di attuazione per le elezioni amministrative.
Il contributo del popolo italiano alla lotta di liberazione.
Estensione ad altre provincie dell'Italia liberata della possibilità di ricevere rimesse in danaro dagli Stati Uniti.
Una smentita ufficiale.
La posizione dei Partiti italiani nei riguardi della situazione interna, attraverso gli editoriali della stampa romana.
La revisione delle sentenze di condanna emesse dal soppresso Tribunale speciale.
Il processo Tilena sarà celebrato in dicembre.
La tutela degli Oliari del Popolo in Puglia.
Una conferenza dell'on. Molé a Reggio Calabria.
Il Sindaco di Cagliari ricevuto dal Presidente del Consiglio.
La Federazione socialista fiorentina per una più intensa partecipazione alla guerra.
Un attentato terroristico in un cinema di Palermo.
Feroria nazista. L'assassinio di due patrioti feriti a Poppi
Sommario della *Gazzetta Ufficiale*.
Quotazioni alla Borsa di Roma.
Quotazioni alla Borsa di Napoli.
Quotazioni alla Borsa di Firenze.
Ufficiali, sottufficiali e soldati dei CC. RR. e della R. Guardia di Finanza rimpatriati recentemente dalla prigionia.

### NAZIONI UNITE

Rapporto di Roosevelt sugli « affitti e prestiti » e sulla loro contropartita.
Dichiarazioni di La Guardia all'assemblea del Congresso delle Organizzazioni Industriali.
La preparazione militare nel periodo post-bellico negli Stati Uniti.
Crowley resta all'Ufficio per le Relazioni economiche con l'Estero.
La Commissione Consultiva per l'Europa e il controllo della Germania.
Eisenhower chiede un raddoppiamento della produzione bellica.
Rappresentanti della Federazione delle Industrie Britanniche si recheranno nei paesi oltremare.
Proposta britannica alla conferenza per l'aviazione.
Un dibattito sugli affari esteri all'Assemblea Consultiva francese.
Telegramma di de Gaulle a Leclerc per la liberazione di Strasburgo.
Dichiarazioni del Ministro Diethelm dopo la liberazione di Strasburgo.
La nomina del Commissario per Strasburgo.
Il generale Henri Giraud fa ritorno a Metz.
Creazione di un organismo in Francia per il mantenimento di relazioni colle Assemblee Alleate.
Funzionari della « Air France » arrestati per tradimento e collaborazionismo.
Ex-sottosegretario francese condannato ai lavori forzati a vita.
La ricostruzione nel territorio russo liberato.
Testo del comunicato russo-jugoslavo sui colloqui Stalin-Subasic.
Il Ministro Spaak di ritorno à Bruxelles.
Un cacciatorpediniere britannico alla Norvegia.
Le fabbriche di industriali collaborazionisti in Jugoslavia saranno confiscate.
I patrioti greci, ossequienti alle disposizioni, disarmeranno.
Mutamenti nel Gabinetto greco.
Dimissioni del Primo Ministro polacco.
La stampa e il rimaneggiamento del Governo cinese.
Gli indocinesi prevedono prossimo il termine delle loro sofferenze.
L'Australia denuncierà i giapponesi colpevoli di atrocità verso prigionieri di guerra.
I congiurati di Oruro saranno processati lunedì.
Le nuove « Superfortezze volanti » americane.
L'Australia ha 347 navi da guerra.

### PAESI NEMICI ED OCCUPATI

Il primo processo celebrato da un Tribunale Militare britannico in territorio tedesco.
Cifre sulla diserzione degli operai stranieri in Germania.
Ennesimo appello all'ormai basso morale tedesco.
La propaganda nazista dello « Herrenvolk » fa macchina indietro.
I giapponesi temono il collasso interno in seguito agli attacchi aerei.
La situazione della mano d'opera esaminata da un economista giapponese.
Le condizioni spaventose di 250.000 norvegesi evacuati dai tedeschi.

### STATI NEUTRALI

Invio di soccorsi turchi per i bambini greci.
Un piroscafo svedese non giunto a destinazione.
Un articolo del Principe Pacelli sui soccorsi americani all'Italia.

## ULTIME NOTIZIE

**Pattuglie alleate avrebbero varcato il Reno.**

LONDRA, 24 novembre (NNU-Reuter) — Un dispaccio della *Reuter* di questa sera informa che pattuglie di ricognizione americane e francesi avrebbero varcato il Reno.

Il dispaccio dice che le pattuglie alleate non sono necessariamente le avanguardie di una grossa puntata oltre il fiume.

**Mommensheim e Saales conquistate**

COMANDO SUPREMO ALLEATO DELLE FORZE DI SPEDIZIONE, 24 novembre (NNU) — Il corrispondente speciale della *Reuter*, Marshall Yarrow, informa questa sera che unità della 7. armata americana hanno occupato oggi Mommensheim, 16 chilometri a nord-ovest di Strasburgo. Nella stessa Strasburgo sono ancora in corso accaniti combattimenti, ma la liberazione della città prosegue rapidamente. Altre unità della 7. armata hanno conquistato Saales di cui, secondo quanto hanno dichiarato alcuni abitanti, le truppe tedesche avevano detto che sarebbe stata un punto strategico della loro linea invernale.

**Il gen. Blaskowitz rimosso dalla carica.**

LONDRA, 24 novembre (NNU) — Un dispaccio della *Associated Press* pervenuto tardi questa notte informa che il gen. Johannes Blaskowitz, secondo notizie ricevute oggi, sarebbe stato rimosso dal comando delle forze tedesche nella Francia orientale dove l'estremità orientale della linea tedesca sta sgretolandosi sotto i colpi dell'offensiva alleata.

1

**Notizie Nazioni Unite** (United Nations News) is an example of occupational propaganda at its best and most effective. Published daily except Sunday by the Rome unit of the Psychological Warfare Branch, Allied Force Headquarters, it was distributed to Italian Government officials, politicians, editors, writers and broadcasters. It specialized in giving straight news, slanted slightly to put Allied activities in the best light possible. Before PWB helped independent, trustworthy Italians set up their own news service ANSA and before commercial press associations began selling news to Italian newspapers, this newspaper's circulation exceeded 10,000 daily.

# ITALIA COMBATTE

TRASPORTATO DALL AVIAZONE ALLEATA — 30 MAGGIO 1944

## ISTRUZIONI

Le notizie e le istruzioni contenute in questo giornale provengono direttamente dal Quartier Generale del Generale Alexander, e vengono trasmesse nel programma de "L'Italia Combatte" dalle stazioni di Bari, Napoli e Palermo.

*L'avanzata alleata ha creato e sta creando situazioni nuove, che possono evolversi da un momento all'altro. I patrioti devono tenersi pronti a ricevere nuove istruzioni. Le trasmissioni di Radio Londra (ore 22,30) e quelle de "L'Italia Combatte" (Radio Bari e Radio Napoli, stessa ora) debbono essere ascoltate attentamente. Per adeguare le istruzioni alle diverse situazioni che si possono creare in vari tratti del territorio ancora occupato, il Quartier Generale del Generale Alexander ha diviso l'Italia invasa in varie zone:*

1. — *Terra di nessuno;*

2. — *Zona che include e circonda Roma;*

3. — *Fascia costiera dal Tevere all'Arno.*

4. — *Appennino centrale,*

5. — *Fascia costiera adriatica da Pescara al Rubicone;*

6. — *Italia settentrionale (a nord della linea Pisa-Rimini)*

*In conseguenza dell'attuale movimento di colonne tedesche, verso il sud, lungo la costa occidentale, sono state impartite nuove istruzioni per i patrioti della 3. zona, e cioè per quelli operanti nella fascia costiera dal Tevere all'Arno. Le istruzioni sono le seguenti:*

1. — *I patrioti di detta zona debbono fare tutto il possibile per ostacolare le comunicazioni nei tratti dove avviene lo spostamento delle truppe tedesche;*

2. — *I patrioti debbono accertare i più minuti particolari sul dislocamento e sullo spostamento delle truppe germaniche. Debbono essere accertati il numero, l'armamento, i nominativi dei reparti, gli itinerari, l'ubicazione e i sistemi di collegamento delle colonne germaniche. Queste notizie sono d'importanza essenziale per i comandi alleati. I patrioti debbono essere in grado di fornirle con la massima precisione quando ne verranno richiesti*

3. — *In conseguenza dei movimenti effettuati dalle truppe germaniche, i patrioti delle zone già sgombrate hanno maggiori possibilità di azione contro i tedeschi e i fascisti che rimangono sul posto. Benchè il tempo per un'azione in massa non sia ancora giunto, è opportuno fin d'ora aumentare l'attività contro i nazifascisti dove questo è possibile in seguito all'allontanamento delle maggiori forze del nemico. Gli attacchi vanno eseguiti oculatamente, senza scoprirsi troppo e senza compromettere la solidità delle organizzazioni che debbono continuare a rafforzarsi e a prepararsi per il momento dell'azione in massa.*

*Vanno controllati con particolare attenzione i movimenti delle seguenti divisioni tedesche: 162. Fanteria (distintivo: una T maiuscola, tagliata in mezzo ad angolo retto da una freccia); 356. Fanteria; 188. Riserva truppe di montagna; 92. Fanteria; Divisione corazzata paracadutisti "Hermann Goering" (distintivo: un quadrante d'orologio con la freccia, e bracciale con la scritta "Hermann Goering").*

*Patrioti, attenti agli ordini e alle istruzioni. Occhi alle spie. Il momento di agire, prima o poi, verrà per tutti.*

## Alpini e Austriaci operano contro i Nazisti

Riportiamo gli ultimi bollettini della resistenza nell'Italia occupata dai tedeschi, già diramati nella quotidiana trasmissione radiofonica. Essi riassumono il valore e la decisione degli Italiani nella lotta contro l'oppressore.

*Bollettino N. 42 del 26 Maggio 1944*

L'ATTIVITA' dei patrioti è stata particolarmente intensa nelle Marche e in Toscana, specie nelle regioni delle Apuane, per reagire alle operazioni nazi-fasciste di rastrellamento.

In uno scontro presso il Lago Maggiore, i fascisti hanno avuto la peggio. 3 militi sono morti, altri sono rimasti feriti.

Una pattuglia di 7 patrioti ha compiuto efficaci atti di sabotaggio contro le linee ferroviarie di Sampierdarena.

*Bollettino N. 43 del 27 Maggio 1944*

UN battaglione di alpini della Divisione "Julia", ha costituito, insieme ad elementi austriaci antinazisti, un forte nucleo di patrioti che ha operato attivamente nella zona di Vittorio Veneto contro il traffico tedesco.

Altri patrioti controllano la zona tra il Lago di Como e il confine svizzero

Data l'intensa attività dei patrioti fra Campomorone e Voltri, i nazifascisti hanno dovuto adottare misure eccezionali di polizia controllando notte e giorno tutte le case. Nonostante ciò, gli atti di sabotaggio e i colpi di mano aumentano.

In seguito all'uccisione di un milite e al ferimento di un altro, nel corso di uno scontro, 13 ostaggi sono stati trucidati a Savona e a Valloria

Sono stati di recente uccisi in combattimento o giustiziati come traditori e spie i seguenti fascisti: Antonio NIZZO, Giuseppe TASSETTI, e l'ex squadrista VILLANI di Torino, Oreste ETERNO di Cocconato; Roberto PIZZI che si era arruolato come sottufficiale nelle S. S. e Osvaldo SCARTIGLIO della 29. Legione della guardia repubblicana.

Un tenente fascista, che tentava di far uso delle armi contro i patrioti, è stato ucciso a Gallarate.

*Bollettino N. 44 del 28 Maggio 1944*

SCADUTO il termine posto dai nazifascisti per la presentazione degli uomini che vivono alla macchia, è risultato che il numero dei patrioti è notevolmente aumentato durante il mese di maggio. L'equipaggiamento del grande esercito volontario che lotta sul fronte sotterraneo della resistenza, viene ora completato, zona per zona, a seconda delle necessità d'impiego.

Parecchi atti di sabotaggio sono stati compiuti lungo la linea ferroviaria tirrenica.

In uno scontro presso Verona sono stati uccisi 5 fascisti. Quattro patrioti catturati vennero successivamente fucilati.

Militi fascisti sono stati giustiziati a Piacenza, Ferrara e Cesena.

*Bollettino N. 45 del 29 Maggio 1944*

LE ferrovie dell'Italia Settentrionale e Centrale, a causa dei continui atti di sabotaggio e degli attacchi compiuti dai patrioti, non sono più in grado di funzionare regolarmente. I treni da Firenze a Roma partono di rado o non partono affatto. Lungo tutto questo tratto l'esercito tedesco deve ora usare soltanto le strade rotabili. Per garantire i necessari rifornimenti alle truppe di Kesserling, è stato di conseguenza mobilitato un gran numero di autotrasporti che non sempre riescono ad evitare le insidie e i colpi di mano dei patrioti.

Dopo aver tagliato le linee telefoniche e telegrafiche, un forte gruppo di patrioti ha circondato una caserma a Pianello Val Tidone, in provincia di Piacenza, domandando la resa dei carabinieri fascisti che la occupavano. Ne è seguito un violento scontro, con perdite da ambo le parti.

Il podestà e il segretario comunale di Melle, in provincia di Cuneo, attivi collaborazionisti dei tedeschi, sono stati rapiti dai patrioti, e sottoposti a processo sommario. Essendo risultato che essi erano responsabili di gravi delitti ai danni dell'esercito di liberazione, sono stati giustiziati.

## Le Forze Armate Italiane in azione

Dalla zona di operazione, il Comando Alleato comunica che il Corpo italiano di liberazione formato da unità regolari dell'Esercito italiano messe dal Maresciallo Badoglio a disposizione del Comandante in capo per combattere contro il comune nemico, è stato in linea durante gli ultimi due mesi.

Durante la battaglia ora in corso, al Corpo italiano di liberazione è stato assegnato il settore sul fianco dell'Ottava Armata. In questi ultimi giorni, le truppe italiane, avanzando su un terreno difficile, conquistavano la località di Picinisco, ad oltre duemila metri d'altezza e coprivano una distanza di circa 20 chilometri dalle posizioni di partenza. L'avanzata continua.

## TUTTI SIANO PRONTI A SCENDERE IN CAMPO

Il Ministro Togliatti, Capo del Partito Comunista Italiano, ha parlato per la seconda volta ai patrioti italiani dal microfono de "L'Italia Combatte"

Dopo aver dichiarato di rivolgersi a tutti i connazionali delle regioni ancora occupate, e specialmente agli amici e ai compagni di Roma, che stanno vivendo nuove ore di febbre sentendo avvicinarsi il momento della liberazione, e dopo aver accennato ai grandi travolgenti successi ottenuti finora dall'offensiva alleata, il Ministro Togliatti ha ricordato che il giorno del crollo totale e definitivo della Germania hitleriana è ormai vicino. Egli ha poi detto: "Questa è per noi tutti, questa è in prima linea per voi, amici e compagni dell'Italia occupata, un'ora di grande responsabilità. E' vicino il momento in cui tutte le vostre forze devono entrare in azione per affrettare il giorno tanto agognato della liberazione di tutta la nostra Patria, e, prima di tutto, della sua capitale immortale, di quella Roma che è oggi, ancora una volta, l'aspirazione, il sogno di tutti i patrioti italiani. Oggi bisogna che *tutti siano pronti a scendere in campo*, in rapporto strettissimo con lo svolgimento stesso delle operazioni militari alleate. L'obbiettivo è precisissimo: Le forze armate hitleriane che si sono gettate sull'Italia, che l'hanno violentata, che hanno intriso il nostro suolo del sangue dei nostri fratelli, devono essere *distrutte*. Ripeto: *devono essere distrutte*. Ciò avverrà in modo inevitabile se al momento opportuno esse saranno schiacciate, da un lato dalla avanzata travolgente delle armate alleate e dall'ancora piccolo ma valoroso Corpo di Liberazione Italiano, e, dall'altro, dalla sollevazione generale delle popolazioni assetate di libertà e di vendetta" Palmiro Togliatti ha incitato tutti gli italiani a preparare, organizzare, inquadrare, disciplinare la sollevazione popolare contro gli oppressori. Egli ha detto: "L'eroe nazionale del popolo nostro, Garibaldi, ci ha dato l'esempio del modo come alcune migliaia di uomini possono, ben diretti e decisi a tutto, dare scacco a unità regolari, liberare e tenere nelle loro mani zone intere di territorio, spostarsi da un luogo all'altro, accendere e tenere accesa in intiere regioni la fiamma della guerra del popolo per la libertà del proprio paese. Oggi noi dobbiamo aggiungere all'esperienza garibaldina l'altra preziosa esperienza del movimento operaio di massa, degli scioperi generali che possono paralizzare nel momento decisivo la vita di città e di regioni intiere, e mettere le truppe dell'invasore in una situazione disperata" Palmiro Togliatti ha poi dichiarato: "Lo so che vi chiamo a una lotta durissima e a un sacrificio. Ma è la Patria stessa che vi rivolge questo appello supremo" E ha così concluso: "L'invasore tedesco dev'essere distrutto. Esso deve sentire ancora una volta, come già parecchie volte gli facemmo sentire nei secoli, che l'Italia non è terra di conquista nè madre di schiavi, ma Patria di un popolo infelice sì, perchè mai è riuscito ad essere pienamente padrone dei suoi destini, ma deciso oggi a conquistarsi per sempre la sua libertà. Nel nome della libertà, dell'Italia e di Roma, al lavoro e alla lotta affinchè la vittoria sia nostra il più presto possibile"

### Ascoltate

**La trasmissione de "L'Italia Combatte", destinata ai patrioti delle terre ancora occupate dai Tedeschi, viene effettuata tutte le sere dalle ore 22.30 alle 23, dalla stazione di Bari sulle lunghezze d'onda di metri 283.3-221 e dalla stazione di Napoli sulla lunghezza d'onda di metri 228-235. Dalle ore 23 alle 23.15 la stessa trasmissione viene effettuata dalla stazione di Palermo sulla lunghezza d'onda di metri 531**

**Lo stesso programma viene ritrasmesso sulla lunghezza d'onda di metri 283.3 dalle ore 7 alle 7.30 di ogni mattina.**

**Italia Combatte fanned the sparks of resistance in Northern Italy for more than a year and a half. The name was also used for a popular radio program beamed into northern Italy from Radio Algiers, Radio Naples, Radio Rome and Radio Florence. From this newspaper and from the radio, the thousands of Italian partisans received their instructions from the Allied commander in Italy.**

กู้บ้าน!
ไมตรีจิตต์จาก
สหรัฐอเมริกา


ที่ ๑๖ เมษายน พ.ศ. ๒๔๘๘ ส่งถึงโดยเครื่องบินอเมริกัน

# ประธานาธิบดี
# โรสเวลต์
# ถึงอนิจจกรรม!

This is a typical American leaflet. Printed in Thai (Siamese), it announces to the people of Thailand the death of President Roosevelt, but reiterates America's determination to crush Japan and Germany.

# ประธานาธิบดีโรสเวลต์ถึงอนิจจกรรม!

★

ประธานาธิบดีโรสเวลต์แห่งสหรัฐอเมริกาได้ถึงแก่กรรมเสียแล้วโดยมิได้คาดฝัน เมื่อวันที่ ๑๒ เมษายน ศกนี้ เนื่องจากเส้นโลหิตในสมองแตก. ทางการอเมริกันได้ประกอบพิธีฝังศพมหาบุรุษผู้นี้เมื่อวันที่ ๑๕ เมษายน. รองประธานาธิบดี แฮรี่ ทรูแมน ได้เข้าปฏิญาณตนรับตำแหน่งประธานาธิบดี ต่อจากท่านโรสเวลต์.

บรรดาผู้นำพรรคการเมือง คณะต่างๆของอเมริกาต่างก็ลงความเห็นสอดคล้องกันว่า อนิจจกรรมของประธานาธิบดี โรสเวลต์ จะไม่ทำให้นโยบายของอเมริกาที่จะเข้าปราบญี่ปุ่นและเยอรมันนี เปลี่ยนไปเลยแม้แต่น้อย.

CTN-3

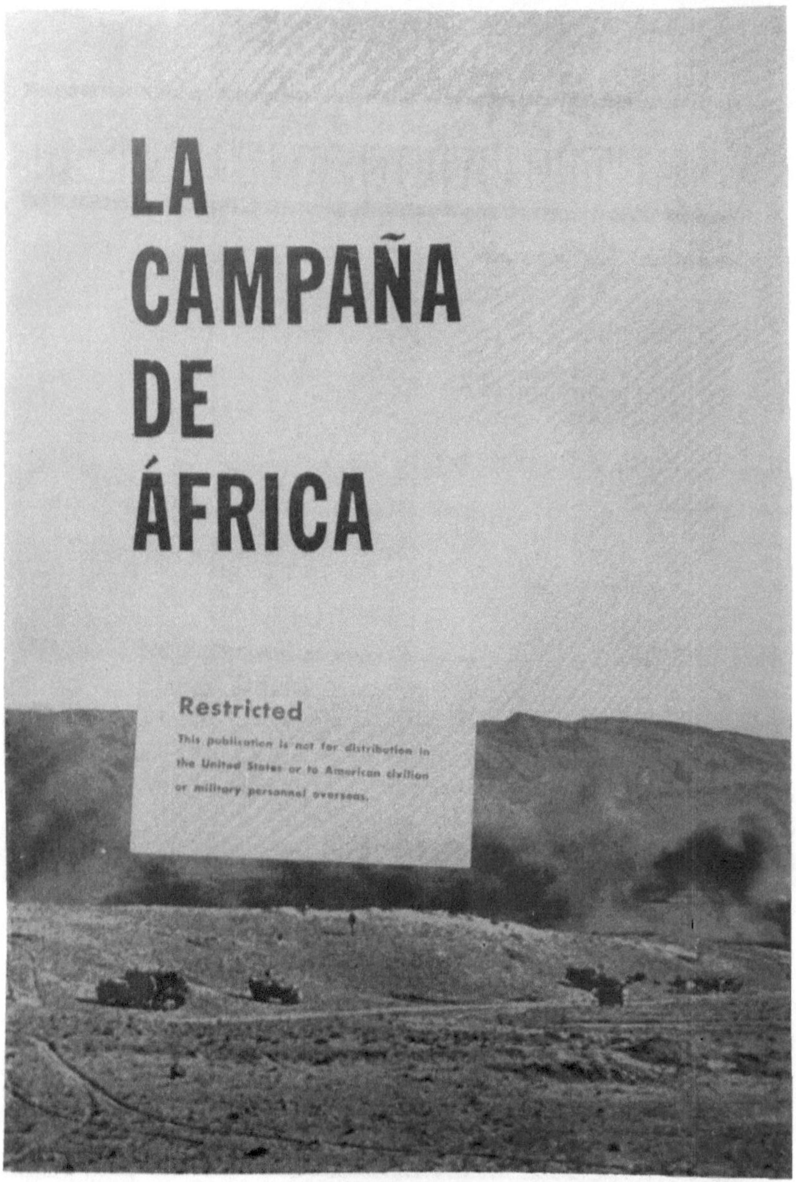


Keeping neutrals neutral was achieved by maintaining their friendship and sympathy for us. In the case of "neutral" Spain, which gave direct and indirect assistance to the Axis, it was necessary to keep her sufficiently scared so that she committed no overt act against the Allies particularly when North Africa was the great Allied military base. This publication helped keep "neutral" Spain as neutral as possible.

While Tokyo Rose was feeding her soft-soapy poison to American soldiers in the Pacific, this was the type of leaflet the Japs were throwing at the Aussies. It was the same "divide and conquer" theme used by the Germans. The leaflet was supposed to show the Aussie soldier that while he was fighting the enemy in New Guinea, American soldiers were having a wonderful time with Australian girls in the homeland.

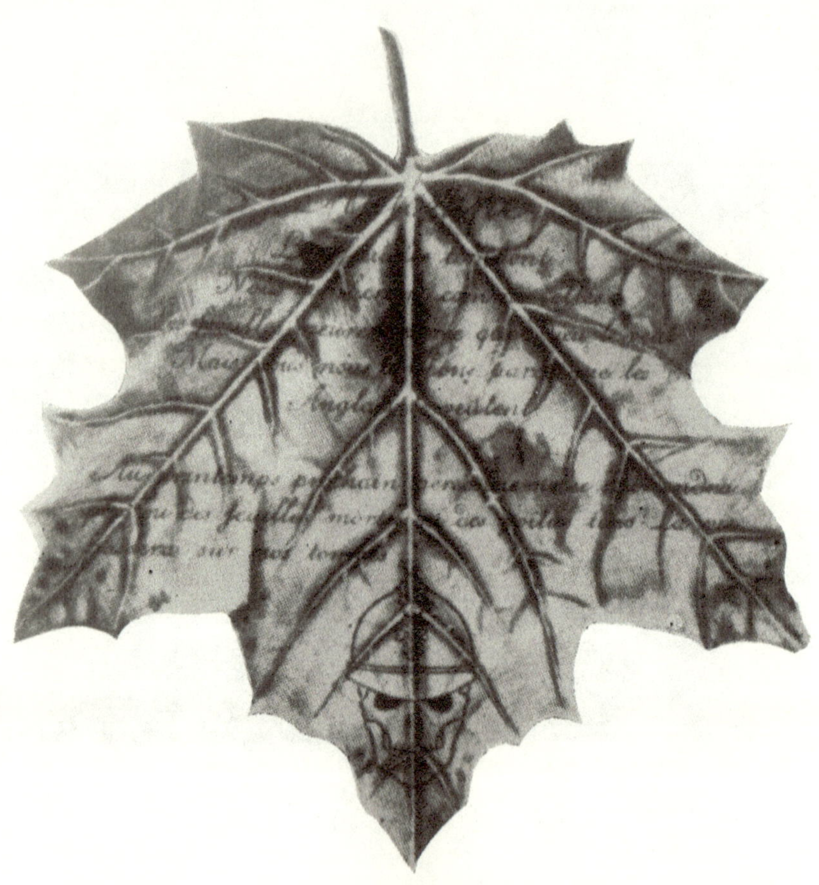

This Nazi job was one of the most effective leaflets ever dropped and did more to break France's will to resist Germany than any other single piece of propaganda. In the shape and color of a green leaf, the leaflet carried the message to the French in the spring of 1940: "If you fight England's battle your soldiers will fall like autumn leaves."

OWI men prepared this leaflet nearly two weeks in advance of Russia's declaration of war on the Japanese. Millions of copies were dropped on the Japanese forces throughout the Pacific.

蘇聯の對日戰參加は日本國民にとつて日本が遂
に全世界の陸軍を相手に絶望的抗戰を餘儀な
く繼續しなければならぬ羽目に陷つたことを意味する。
露西亞を一擧に席卷せんとしたあの精鋭を誇
りし獨逸軍及其の猪突的進攻作戰の首魁者
たる彼の軍國主義者ヒットラーの末路は諸君
の良く知る處であらう。即ち東部戰線に在りし
全獨逸軍も西亞東歐の豪、蘇聯の反攻に際會
して結局は殲滅の憂目に會つたと云ふ事も諸君
の腦裏に深く刻み込まれた事實である筈だ。
苦戰敢鬪數年、遂に獨軍制覇の偉業を確立
した蘇聯軍も歐州戰の終焉に伴ひ現在遙かに
戰前に優る數的、質的陸軍武容を回復充實
し遂に對日聯合戰線に一役買つて出たのである。
聯合國の全面的日本進攻作戰を目前に控へそれ
に伴ふ日本の必然的なる徹底的壞滅を前に日本
國民の採るべき途——
即ち美しき祖國日本を慘澹たる戰禍より未然
に救ふ唯一の途が何であるかと云ふことも諸君は良く
知つて居る筈だ!

144-J-1

**ATTENTION AMERICAN SOLDIERS!**

# I CEASE RESISTANCE

THIS LEAFLET GUARANTEES HUMANE TREATMENT TO ANY JAPANESE DESIRING TO CEASE RESISTANCE. TAKE HIM IMMEDIATELY TO YOUR NEAREST COMMISSIONED OFFICER.

*By Direction of the Commander in Chief.*

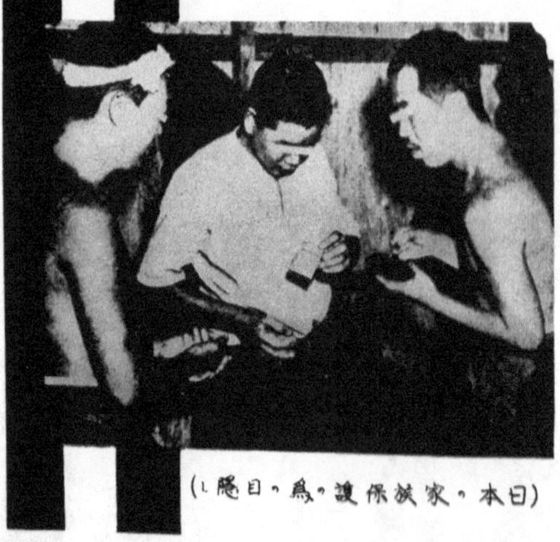

(日本の家族保護の爲目隠し)

上の英文の内容は「この人は最早敵でなく國際條約により生命・衣食住は勿論医療等が完全に保証さるべき者なり」と云ふ意味が書かれて居る

左圖は既に當方に来て居られる諸君の戰友の一部

This was the push over the precipice for the Japanese soldier. The leaflet was thrown to Japs, who were ready to surrender. The lines hiding the eyes of the Japs was to prevent their identification by other Japanese soldiers who received the leaflet. The picture caption states: "This man is no longer an enemy. According to International Law, he is guaranteed personal safety, clothes, food, quarters, and medical attention." The rest of the leaflet, addressed to officers and men of the Japanese Army, tells them they are foolish to die in a hopeless struggle when it is really their duty to preserve their lives "'and help rebuild the future of Japan." Practically all leaflets addressed to the Japs repeated this theme.

# 日本軍将兵諸君

我々は諸君の今迄に於ける善戦に對し衷心より敬意を表するものである。

然しながら我か軍としては飽く迄此の戦争に勝ち抜く爲には既往作戰の如く物凄き砲爆撃及優秀な科學兵器並びに我が各将兵の緊密なる協力に依り確實に勝利を得んとするものである。

諸君は日本軍の勝利を信じ住みなれた故里を幾千里も離れた異郷に来て初めて日本軍飛行機及兵器が聯合軍のに匹敵せざるを痛感したであらう。

我が艦隊及空軍の活躍により台湾以南及び太平洋方面の制空權及び制海權は既に我が手に歸した。　現在の戰況で御承知の通り今後の戰闘も到底勝目がないのは明かである。　然し戰況がかくも悪化したのは勿論諸君等の責任ではなく實に軍首脳部の一大失策責任と言はねばならぬ。

この勝目なき絶望的な戰闘に於て諸君等の爲すべき事は果して徒らに無益の死を急ぐ事であらうか。　亦日本の将来の爲それが一番得策であらうか。

死は易く生は難しである、将来日本再建の爲諸君等は生を全うし強く正しく生きる道を講ずるのは寧ろ目下諸君に課せられたる唯一の義務責任ではなからうか。

ソロモン、ニユーギニア戰線に於ける諸君の戰友は無益の流血を打ち切る事は正にして邪に非らずと大悟し飜然再建日本の爲めに努力せんと決心し立ったのである。

諸君の参考の一端となれば幸ひである。

(出来ればこの紙を木の枝にはさみそれを手に持ちて両手を揚げ我が方に接近し来られ我が将兵に會へば恐れず安心して手真似に従へば良い)

# PSYCHOLOGICAL WARFARE BRANCH

## U.S. ARMY FORCES, PACIFIC AREA

## APO 500

LEAFLET: Red Army Strikes

LANGUAGE: Japanese

DESIGNATION: 144-J-1

TARGET: Japanese homeland

REMARKS: Art shows symbolic Russian and American soldier shaking hands above Japan. Caption reads: "Inspiring Handclasp."

---

(The following is a paraphrase of the Japanese text)

RED ARMY STRIKES

The powerful Soviet Union has now joined the war against Japan. This means that Japan will now be compelled to meet much of the combined might of the entire world.

The fate that befell the German Army when it set out to overwhelm Russia is well known. The Russians not only stopped the invasion of the greatest army ever created, but the Red Army counter-offensive swept the Nazi Army back to Berlin and total defeat.

Despite heavy casualties, the Red Army is now at the peak of its strength both in men and arms. With its great fighting spirit, this battle-tested army has joined the forces aligned against Japan.

Surrounded by a ring of steel, the Japanese people MUST take action to avoid the utter destruction of their country.

Will you continue to allow the militarists to drag your ancestral country to utter ruin?

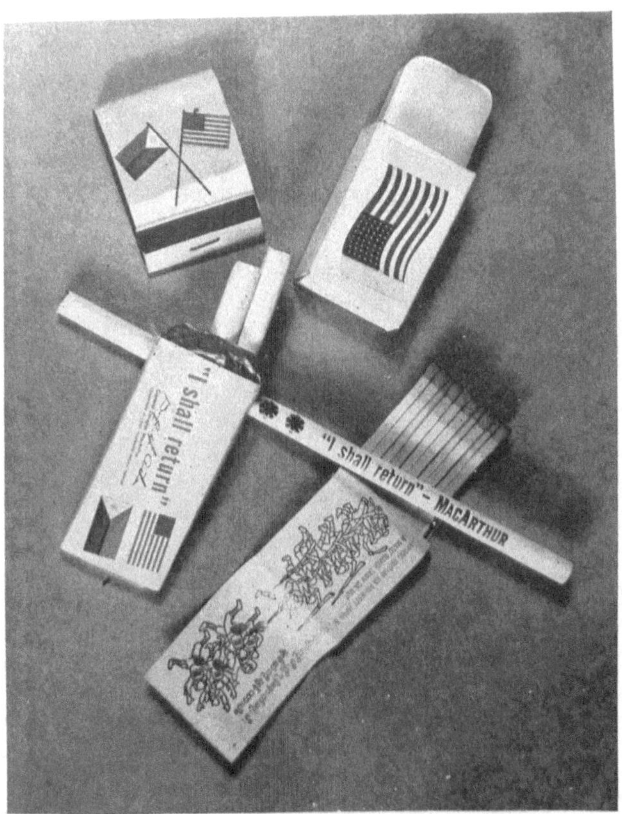


The pencil and the cigarette packet were dropped on the Filipino guerrillas and smuggled into the Islands by submarine. The slogan, "I shall return," was most effective although many editorial writers felt it was a display of ego. On the contrary it helped burn the fire of resistance in the guerrillas until MacArthur did return. The open book of matches helped the Burmese offer resistance to the Japs. The illustration shows American troops chasing the Japs. The soap at the right was an important gift both psychologically and practically

# Passierschein

Der deutsche Soldat, der diesen Passierschein vorzeigt, benutzt ihn als Zeichen seines ehrlichen Willens, sich zu ergeben. Er ist zu entwaffnen. Er muß gut behandelt werden. Er hat Anspruch auf Verpflegung und, wenn nötig, ärztliche Behandlung. Er wird so bald wie möglich aus der Gefahrenzone entfernt.

OBERBEFEHLSHABER
der alliierten Expeditions-Armeen

*Englische Übersetzung nachstehend. Sie dient als Anweisung an die alliierten Vorposten.*

# SAFE CONDUCT

The German soldier who carries this safe conduct is using it as a sign of his genuine wish to give himself up. He is to be disarmed, to be well looked after, to receive food and medical attention as required, and to be removed from the danger zone as soon as possible.

SUPREME COMMANDER,
Allied Expeditionary Force

From a rather crude beginning, the Allied surrender leaflet ended the war looking like a cross between gilt edge bonds and a college diploma. This is how the **Passierschein** or safe conduct pass looked when the last Nazi had surrendered in Europe. The wording, however, remained pretty much the same throughout the war, only the quality of printing improved.

*"Tell them leaflet people th' krauts ain't got time fer readin' today."*

(Reprinted by special permission of the United Feature Syndicate)

**Bill Mauldin, who is really as good a soldier as he is a cartoonist and mouthpiece for the combat infantryman, made an accurate appraisal of the average American soldier's attitude toward "paper bullets." When the American soldier saw the "kraut" prisoners come in by the thousands, he became "the confetti soldier's" best friend.**

# Landser-post

## Für die Deutschen Soldaten in Südfrankreich

Von den Vereinten Nationen

« Wenn durch die Hilfsmittel der Regierungsgewalt ein Volkstum dem Untergang entgegengefuehrt wird, dann ist die Rebellion eines jeden Angehoerigen eines solchen Volkes nicht nur Recht, sondern Pflicht. » Hitler « Mein Kampf » S.104

Jahrgang 1944, Nummer 26

# REVOLUTION DER DEUTSCHEN GENERAELE

## Aufruf der Generaele zur Aktion

LONDON. — Freitag in den fruehen Morgenstunden wurde folgender Aufruf deutscher Generaele auf der Mittelwelle des Reichssenders Frankfurt vernommen:

« In der Vergangenheit haben wir Augenblicke gekannt, in denen einzelne Offiziere, die sich ihrer hoeheren Pflichten gegen unser Vaterland bewusst waren, mutige Handlungen unternahmen und sich weigerten, verbrecherische Befehle ihrer Vorgesetzten auszufuehren. Der Augenblick ist gekommen, in dem allein die gemeinsame Aktion mutiger, gefahrverachtender Offiziere unser geliebtes Vaterland retten kann.

Wir tragen Auszeichnungen fuer Tapferkeit, aber die einzige Auszeichnung, die wir erringen muessen, ist die, die Verbrechen, welche wir im Namen Hitlers begangen haben, wieder gut zu machen. Wir haben Verbrechen aus Angst vor der Gestapo begangen; diese Feigheit koennen wir uns niemals verzeihen.

Ein Mann traegt das Kainszeichen, sein Name ist Hitler!

Kameraden, wir werden die Gestapo nicht laenger dulden!

Wollt Ihr die Verantwortung fuer die Missetaten der Gestapo tragen? Nein! Erhebt die Waffen in klarer Erkenntnis dessen, was auf dem Spiele steht! Schliesst die Reihen! Alle fuer Einen, Einer fuer alle! Vorwaerts! »

FRANCAIS, passez ce journal à un soldat allemand

German prisoners acknowledged that the first news of the attempt on Hitler's life was from Allied sources like this issue of the Landser-post published by PWB for German soldiers in Southern France, where leaflets of this type swept the coast for American and French troops on August 15, 1944.

Landser-post

# DIE FUENFTE FRONT

Am 20. Juli wurde ein Attentat gegen Hitler unternommen. Verschiedene Mitglieder seiner engeren Umgebung wurden verletzt; doch Hitler selber erhielt, nach deutschen Nachrichten, nur oberflaechliche Verwundungen.

Dieser Anschlag soll von einer Gruppe hoeherer deutscher Offiziere geplant und von Oberst Graf von Stauffenberg ausgefuehrt worden sein. Die fuer Deutschlands Befreiung vom Nazijoch kaempfenden deutschen Offiziere haben sich gegen die Partei empoert und sich in einem Aufruf an all die gewandt, die in zwoelfter Stunde Deutschland vom Untergang retten wollen.

Hitler hat Massnahmen zur Entfesselung des Buergerkrieges in Deutschland getroffen. Himmler wurde zum Befehlshaber der Heimatwehr ernannt und Generaloberst Stumpf zum Kommandanten der neu geschaffenen Luftwaffenverbaende, die in Hitlers Namen deutsche Staedte bombardieren sollen. Ferner fordert Hitler alle Deutschen, sowohl Zivilisten als auch Soldaten, auf, den Befehlen der Generaele nicht zu folgen und sich bei jeder Anordnung erst zu versichern, dass sie auch wirklich von Himmler kommt.

Nach Hitler sprachen am deutschen Rundfunk Goering fuer die Luftwaffe und Doenitz fuer die Flotte. Fuer die Armee sprach niemand.

Wie auch der Aufstand der Generaele ausgehen mag, so hat doch diese mutige Tat der Welt bewiesen, dass es trotz elfjaehrigen Gestapo-Terrors in Deutschland noch verantwortungsbewusste Maenner gibt, die nichts fuerchten, wenn es gilt, Deutschland zu befreien. Niemand weiss besser als diese Generaele, dass Nazideutschland den Krieg verloren hat.

Sie haben sich erhoben, als Vorposten der neuen deutschen Befreiungsarmee, die durch den Sturz der verbrecherischen Nazifuehrer noch retten wollen, was zu retten ist. Sie haben die fuenfte Front geschaffen, die Front, in die sich alle ihrer Verantwortung bewussten Deutschen einreihen muessen und aus der ein neues Deutschland hervorgehen wird.

Die Revolution der deutschen Generaele mag fehlgeschlagen sein, die Revolution des deutschen Volkes wird gelingen.

25/28

# Frontpost

AUSGABE SÜD

Nummer 77 — Nachrichtenblatt für deutsche Soldaten — 31 Oktober 1944

## Deutsche 15. Armee auf die Maas zurückgeworfen

«General Montgomery hat die Schlacht von Westholland gewonnen.» Das ist zusammengefasst die allgemeine Ansicht der alliierten Militärsachverständigen über die Lage im nördlichen Abschnitt der Westfront.

Wieder hat eine deutsche Armee, mit einem breiten Strom im Rücken und ohne ausreichende Fliegerdeckung, ihre Stellungen zu lange halten müssen. Im August erlitt die deutsche 7. Armee überaus schwere Verluste bei dem Versuch, die Seine zu überschreiten. Heute fallen Teile der deutschen 15. Armee, etwa 40 000 Mann der Schätzung nach, auf die drei ihnen noch zur Verfügung stehenden Maasübergänge zurück oder versuchen, unter andauernden Fliegerangriffen den Fluss auf Fähren zu überqueren.

Alliierte Verbände, die die deutschen Verteidigungsstellungen durchbrochen haben, haben am 29. Oktober Breda und am 30. Roosendaal und Oosterhuit genommen. Nördlich der letztgenannten Stadt haben Verbände der englischen 2. Armee sich der Maas bis auf 2 km genähert und halten die deutschen Truppen bei ihrem Rückzug über den Fluss unter Werferfeuer. Alliierte Bomber und Jäger greifen fortgesetzt die deutschen Kolonnen an.

Weiter westlich haben kanadische Truppen nach der Besetzung von Südbeveland 6 000 deutsche Soldaten von den annähernd 11 000 in Südbeveland und auf Walcheren zurückgebliebenen, als Gefangene eingebracht. Aus dem letzten deutschen Kessel südlich der Schelde, der rasch seiner Auflösung entgegengeht, wurden weitere 7 000 Deutsche gefangen genommen. Nur noch die Geschützstellungen von Vlissingen auf der überfluteten Insel Walcheren sind zum Schweigen zu bringen, um den unbeschädigten Hafen von Antwerpen für die Benutzung durch die Alliierten freizumachen.

Eine deutsche Gegenoffensive gegen den Ostabschnitt des englischen Frontvorsprunges, bei der unter anderm 2 Panzerdivisionen eingesetzt wurden, brachte keine nennenswerten Geländegewinne und konnte zum Stehen gebracht werden. Raketenfeuernde Typhoon-Jäger flogen besonders wirkungsvolle Angriffe gegen deutsche Truppenansammlungen, Flossbrücken und Fähren.

Auf dem Südabschnitt der Westfront haben amerikanische Truppen nach heftigen Kämpfen Maizières bei Metz besetzt.

## *Feldmarschall Paulus*

### *„Deutschlands einziger Ausweg - los von Hitler"*

«Es gibt jetzt nur noch einen Weg, der das deutsche Volk aus der Aussichtslosigkeit seiner Lage herausführt: Trennung von Hitler.» So äusserte sich Generalfeldmarschall Paulus, Befehlshaber der deutschen 6. Armee bei Stalingrad, am 28. Oktober im Moskauer Rundfunk.

«Es ist eine infame Lüge», sagte Paulus, «zu behaupten, dass deutsche Soldaten in russischer Gefangenschaft unmenschlich behandelt werden. Wahr ist vielmehr, dass sie menschlich und gerecht behandelt werden, trotz der Greueltaten, die die SS im Osten verübt hat.

Im Gefühl der Pflicht, ihrem Volk zu helfen, haben sich Hunderttausende deutscher Kriegsgefangener in Russland, darunter Tausende von Offizieren und über dreissig Generäle, der Bewegung «Freies Deutschland» angeschlossen. Himmler weiss sehr wohl, dass es sich

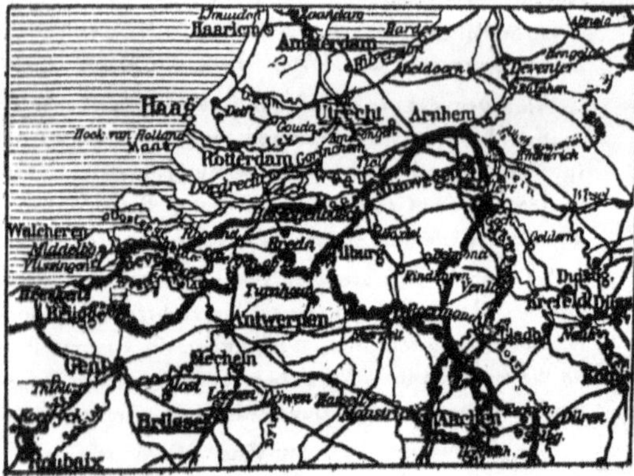


FRONTPOST was one of the most successful Allied propaganda enterprises. This issue tells German soldiers on the Italian front that German 15th Army has been badly beaten in western Holland.

*(TRANSLATION)*

No. 77 — Newspaper for German troops — October 31st, 1944

# German 15th Army pushed towards Maas crossings

« Field Marshal Montgomery has won the battle of Western Holland. » This is how Allied experts sum up the situation on the northern sector of the Western Front.

Once again a German army, with a broad river at its back and inadequate air cover, was left to hold its positions for too long. In August, the German 7th Army suffered crippling losses in attempting to retreat across the Seine. To-day, elements of the German 15th Army estimated at 40,000 men are racing towards three crossings of the river Maas still available to them, or endeavouring to cross the river by ferry under air attack.

Allied forces which broke through the German defences on the 29th Oct. took Breda and on the 30th Roosendaal and Oosterhuit. North of the last-named town, troops of the British 2nd Army have reached points only 2 km from the Maas and are mortaring German troops escaping across the river. Allied bombers and fighters are continuously attacking retraiting German columns.

Further West, Canadian and British forces which overran South Beveland have taken prisoner 6000 of the approximately 11,000 German troops left behind in South Beveland and Walcheren. A further 7 000 Germans have been captured in the last German pocket south of the Scheldt, which is rapidly being reduced. Only the guns at Flishing, on the submerged island of Walcheren, remain to be reduced before the undamaged port of Antwerp is clear for Allied use.

A counter-offensive launched by German forces including two armoured divisions against the eastern sector of the British salient was brought to a stop without significant gains. RAF rocket firing Typhoon fighters were particularly effective in attacking German troop concentrations, pontoon bridges and barges.

On the southern sector of the Western Front, American troops after severe fighting occupied Maizieres, near Metz.

# *Field Marshal Paulus:*

### *„Germany's only way out - away from Hitler!"*

« In the present hopeless war situation the German people has only one way out — to separate from Hitler », Field Marshal Paulus, former German 6th Army Commander at Stalingrad, said over the Moscow Radio on the 28th Oct.

Paulus also said:

« It is an infamous lie to say that the Russians maltreat German prisoners of war. The truth is that they are treated well and humanely, in spite of the cruelties committed in the East by the SS.

« As a duty to their own people, hundreds of thousands of German prisoners of war in Russia, including thousands of officers and more than 30 generals, have joined the movement « Free Germany ». « Himmler knows very well these men are not dishono-

# IV
# FRANCE: VICTIM OF WORDS

One bright spring morning in 1940, Parisians leaving their homes to go about the business of the day were startled by the sight they beheld in their streets. There were bright green leaves everywhere. But they weren't ordinary leaves.

Sometime during the night, while Parisians slept soundly, secure in the thought that the Maginot line was impenetrable, German planes had unloaded the leaves on Paris.

The "leaves" were actually Nazi leaflets—a perfect green paper replies of leaves—bearing the message: "If you fight England's battle, your soldiers will fall like autumn leaves!"

The Parisians were badly shaken. They had been subjected to the so-called "phony war" since the previous September. The inactivity at the front as the French sat in the Maginot line and the Germans relaxed in the Siegfried line of Westwall, had shattered the nerves of the French populace.

During these months of military inactivity, the French people had been saturated by poison, manufactured by Dr. Joseph Goebbels, Nazi propaganda chief, and fed them under one camouflage of another by French traitors who carefully spread defeatism by such remarks as: "What's the use?" and "The English are fighting to the last Frenchman!" These phrases had been repeated thousands of times and as Hitler himself has said: "The bigger the lie and the more often repeated, the bigger the belief."

What the French people did not realize until it was too late was that Goebbels and Hitler were not interested in beginning any military campaign until the French had been softened up sufficiently for the big kill. The success the Nazis achieved in this "phony war," which was actually psychological warfare at its deadliest, amazed even the Nazis.

Colonel General Jodi, Chief of the Operations Staff of the German High Command, told American intelligence officers in 1945 that the unexpectedly swift victory over France and Great Britain's continuation of the war found the General Staff unprepared for an invasion of England. That inability to follow up their psychological and military victories was one of Germany's seven fatal errors, according to General of the Army George C. Marshall.

A German double-dealer named Otto Abetz was the Nazi propagandist, more than any other, who was the leading termite in France's defeat.

Before the French Government had taken official notice of Abetz's activities he had set up a tight, spiderweb network of native Frenchmen working in behalf of the Nazis. Most of these thought they were patriots because they were working to purge France of such imagined enemies as Jews, Socialists, Communists.

They found out too late that they were working for the Nazis.

The basis of Abetz's deadly group was rumor-mongering, specializing in creating distrust of the French Government and its leaders. Newspapers were corrupted; newspapermen were bought; book publishers were subsidized and Abetz secured a number of willing recruits in the French salons where he enticed French society women with flattery and plenty of money.

Abetz was expelled from France before the declaration of war, but he had done his work well. His organization worked automatically, in burrowing, like busy beavers, into the heart of France and gnawing away at France's will to resist. One of the oft-repeated lies, the rumor-mongers repeated, asked: "Where are the British troops?"

No answer was given immediately, but with this pressing question on the minds and tongues of most Frenchmen, Goebbels saw to it that they got an answer, although the answer was the usual Nazi whopper.

Millions of leaflets showing a vivid drawing of tired and dirty French soldiers in forward positions while a French woman lay in the arms of a British soldier, was the answer Goebbels provided. It never occurred to the excitable Frenchmen that this might be a falsity. With no fighting and no decision, he allowed the poison to overrun his better judgment.

The French soldiers whiling the time away inside the Maginot line were not overlooked by the canny Nazi propagandists. The Germans gave the French soldiers daily loudspeaker talks emanating from the Siegfried line. There were concerts too of popular French tunes. French soldiers were invited to come out of the Maginot line and wash their clothes in safety. After repeating the invitation several times, the Germans were rewarded by the sight of French soldiers who accepted the bid.

The French soldiers came out of the line and did their laundry unmolested by bullets or shell fire. But "paper bullets" and words were fired at them. German loudspeakers told the French soldiers:

"See, French comrades, we weren't fooling you. We told you to wash your clothes in safety and we have kept our word. We have no quarrel with you. You are our European brothers. We love you very dearly. We want no war with you. It is your leaders who have betrayed you into fighting a war for hated England. Continue your washing unmolested. Here, listen to this pretty French song!"

In the briskness of the winter air of 1939-1940 the French soldiers' will to fight evaporated like his breath.

The loudspeaker talks were not all. These idle French soldiers with nothing but the Nazi messages on their minds were recipients of "poison pen" letters. Postmarked from their home towns, French soldiers would receive postcards signed "A Friend," telling them that their wives were being unfaithful. Sometimes the adulterers would be identified as British soldiers.

The postcard's message would vary. "A Friend" would report that a soldier's children were hungry and could get no food because it had been requisitioned by the army. Or the postcard writer, usually a Frenchman working for the Germans, would report that the soldier's children were ill and without medical attention because all physicians had been called into military service.

Then to make the blow at the morale of the inactive French soldier complete, the German loudspeaker would say:

"Regiment number so-and-so (the exact regimental number would be given), you thought you were going to be relieved tomorrow but the plans have been changed. You will stay in your positions for another two weeks."

Or a new relieving regiment would be greeted this way:

"Regiment Number so-and-so (again the exact number was given), we are so sorry you had such bad weather on your march to relieve such and such a regiment" (and again the exact number was given).

And it was not unusual for the German loudspeaker to announce:

"Tomorrow you will be inspected by the President of the French Republic."

Aggravating this military insecurity was the constant repetition by the enemy loudspeakers stressing the absence of British troops in the Maginot line and their conspicuous presence—with French women, of course—in the rear echelons.

Meanwhile, the civilians were receiving their share of the poison—like the leaves. Civilians frequently were warned by other leaflets that a definite Sunday was to be the last peaceful one Parisians would ever know. On the Monday following the specifically named Sunday, the Germans would stage a small, token air raid on Paris. This confirmed to the French how right the enemy was.

That was not all in store for the hapless French. After the Maginot line was outflanked psychologically, it was easily outflanked militarily and the German hordes descended on a petrified, panic-stricken France. The great myth of the German army's invincibility lay heavy on the minds of the French in addition to the other poison already there.

Then came the screaming Stukas. They rattled French nerves completely. Then Abetz's plan went into operation for the coordination of psychological warfare with actual military warfare. It was that phase of psychological warfare called "the strategy of terror."

Abetz's stooges threw France into a panic with their fake telephone instructions to scores of French mayors. Mayors would be telephoned to and a voice identifying itself as a high military authority would warn the mayor that his town was about to be bombed by the enemy and ordered him to send his people onto the roads. This happened scores of times until France was one huge, choked roadblock. The retreating French army couldn't retreat because of the roads choked with civilians, and reinforcements couldn't reinforce for the same reason.

To add to the confusion, German pilots scoured the choked roads and deliberately machine-gunned the helpless civilians. Even in places where not a single French soldier was within miles of the spot, the Germans deliberately strafed, adding to the terror.

That kind of psychological warfare has a carry-over effect, putting fear into the hearts of civilians. This fear is transferred to the period of occupation. The Germans knew that fear-smitten, docile populations are always easier to handle.

To make certain that their overwhelmingly successful psychological defeat of France stuck, the Germans took full advantage of the British evacuation of Dunkirk, when a sizeable part of the British Expeditionary Force was saved, but without equipment. The Nazi propaganda used, to magnify this catastrophe, was:

"France stands alone and will bear all the sacrifices, while England is safe and perfectly willing to fight to the last Frenchman."

Again the Germans omitted a very important fact: the Nazis were subjecting England to saturation blitz air warfare and this later was followed by the fiendish buzz bombing.

It can be truly said that France had been crucified on the broadcasting rod of a short-wave radio antenna, the tip of which had been poisoned by rumor, and the spikes had been driven by "100 percent French," who had done Hitler's work so effectively.

Hitler's words in "Mein Kampf" drove home the lesson:

"Let the enemy defeat himself!"

# V
# PROPAGANDA: A GERMAN NATIONAL DISH

Propaganda is as realistic as a bleeding wound.

Propaganda became very important to the combat soldier because to him it was a matter of life or death. Ten fewer of the enemy shooting at him, because those ten believed a leaflet and surrendered, meant his very existence to the foxhole soldier.

The mere fact that a leaflet, or a radio broadcast, or a well-planted but sinister rumor, is "just a lot of talk" is no excuse for ignoring its deadly effect. The childhood chant, "Sticks and stones will break my bones but names will never harm me," should be deposited in the nearest ashcan along with the idea that America is safe from overseas aggression because it is "protected" on the east and west by two big oceans.

General Dwight D. Eisenhower put it neatly when he reminded a New York dinner audience: "It is sixteen hours by plane from this spot to my headquarters in Frankfurt."

What America's B-29s did to Japan in their 16-hour, 3,000-mile round trips between their Pacific bases and the Japanese home islands, should be a

## An die

# ZIVILBEVÖLKERUNG

## Frankfurts am Main und Mannheim - Ludwigshafens

IHR wohnt in einem der wichtigsten Kriegsindustriegebiete Deutschlands.

Die Kriegsindustrien Frankfurts und Mannheim-Ludwigshafens werden von jetzt ab einem erbarmungslosen Bombardement ausgesetzt.

Es ist aber nicht das Ziel der Alliierten, das deutsche Volk zu vernichten. Vernichtet werden soll die deutsche Kriegsmaschine

**Der alliierte Oberbefehlshaber erlässt daher folgende Bekanntmachung:**

**1. Die Bekanntmachung gilt für alle Teile des Stadtkreises Frankfurt am Main, einschliesslich folgender Vororte: NIEDERURSEL, HEDDERNHEIM, ESCHERSHEIM, ECKENHEIM, GINNHEIM, PREUNGESHEIM, SECKBACH, FECHENHEIM, BÜRGEL, OFFENBACH, OBERRAD, NIEDERRAD, GRIESHEIM, RÖDELHEIM, HAUSEN, PRAUNHEIM.**

**2. Die Bekanntmachung gilt für die Stadtkreise Mannheim-Ludwigshafen, einschliesslich folgender Vororte: SANDHOFEN, WALDHOF, KÄFERTAL,WALLSTADT, FEUDENHEIM, SECKENHEIM, NECKARAU, MUNDENHEIM, RHEINGÖNHEIM, MUTTERSTADT, FRIESENHEIM, OGGERSHEIM, OPPAU, EDESHEIM, FRANKENTAL.**

**3. Diese Gebiete sind jetzt Kampfzonen. An alle Bewohner dieser namentlich aufgeführten Gebiete ergeht hiermit die Aufforderung, sich selbst und ihre Familien unverzüglich ausserhalb der Kampfzone in Sicherheit zu bringen.**

**4. Besonders wird darauf hingewiesen, dass in den oben genannten Gebieten von nun an weder Bunker noch Unterstände Sicherheit gewähren können.**

**Euer Leben hängt von der sofortigen Ausführung dieser Anweisungen ab. Handelt sofort! Heraus aus der Gefahrenzone! Heraus aus dem Krieg!**

Dwight D. Eisenhower

**DWIGHT D. EISENHOWER,**
**General,**
**Oberbefehlshaber der alliierten Streitkräfte**

**S.H.A.E.F., 17. März 1945**

**DEUTSCHE ARBEITER! Gebt diese Bekanntmachung des alliierten Oberbefehlshabers sofort an Eure ausländischen Arbeitskollegen weiter!**

Psychological warfare working five ways—on the Germans and their slave labor from France, Czechslovakia, Poland and Italy—is illustrated in this leaflet to frighten all five groups away from German war plants. It worked. In World War II we were attacking German civilian morale which was blamed by the German High Command for Germany's loss of World War I.

*TRANSLATION OF WG.48*

## To the

# CIVIL POPULATION

## of Frankfurt on Main and Mannheim-Ludwigshafen

YOU live in one of Germany's most important areas of war industry.

The whole armament industry of Frankfurt and Mannheim-Ludwigshafen from now on will be subjected to a merciless bombardment.

But the Allies are determined to destroy not the German people, but the German war machine. For this reason the Supreme Commander has issued the following warning.

**1. The warning applies to all parts of Frankfurt am Main including the following suburbs: NIEDERURSEL, HEDDERNHEIM, ESCHERSHEIM, ECKENHEIM, GINNHEIM, PREUNGSHEIM, SECKBACH, FECHENHEIM, BÜRGEL, OFFENBACH, OBER-RAD, NIEDERRAD, GRIESHEIM, RÖDELHEIM, HAUSEN, PRAUNHEIM.**

**2. The warning applies to the town of Mannheim-Ludwigshafen including the following suburbs: SANDHOFEN, WALDHOF, KÄFTERTAL, WALLSTADT, FEUDENHEIM, SECKENHEIM, NECKARAU, MUNDENHEIM, RHEINGÖNHEIM, MUTTER-STADT, FRIESENHEIM, OGGERSHEIM, OPPAU, ESHEIM, FRANKENTAL.**

**3. These districts are now combat areas. Every inhabitant of the above named districts is hereby warned to remove himself and his family immediately to a safe place outside the battle area.**

**4. You are specifically advised that from now on, no shelter or refuge within the above named districts can be considered safe.**

**Your life depends upon the immediate execution of these orders. Act now ! Out of the battle areas ! Out of the war !**

Dwight D. Eisenhower

**DWIGHT D. EISENHOWER,**
**General,**
**Supreme Commander, Allied Expeditionary Force.**

**March 17th, 1945.**

**FOREIGN WORKERS ! Live for your family and country. Refuse to die working in Germany.**

...Général D... Expeditionnaires Alliées

**AUX TRAVAILLEURS FRANÇAIS DANS LES REGIONS DE FRANCFORT-SUR-MAIN ET DE MANNHEIM-LUDWIGSHAFEN**

Le Commandant Suprême vous a avisé jusqu'ici, ainsi que tous les autres travailleurs etrangers en Allemagne occidentale, de ne pas vous laisser evacuer, mais de trouver un refuge sûr dans les environs de l'endroit où vous travaillez et là d'attendre les armées alliées. Il vous adresse maintenant de nouvelles instructions spéciales qui s'appliquent à ceux d'entre vous qui se trouvent dans les regions de Francfort-sur-Main et de Mannheim-Ludwigshafen.

1) Les industries de guerre vont être detruites. C'est-à-dire que toute la region de Francfort-sur-Main et de Mannheim-Ludwigshafen va devenir un lieu de mort.

2) Le Commandant Suprême avise donc tous les travailleurs étrangers dans les régions mentionnees plus haut, de quitter leur lieu de travail et leur logements immédiatement et de se réfugier dans l'endroit le plus sûr qu'ils pourront trouver dans les campagnes avoisinantes, et d'y rester jusqu'à ce que la bataille soit passée.

3) Le Commandant Suprême précise que ces instructions ne s'appliquent pas aux travailleurs étrangers qui se trouvent dans d'autres régions. Elles s'adressent seulement aux travailleurs etrangers qui so trouvent à Francfort-sur-Main ou dans sa banlieue: NIEDERURSEL, HEDDERNHEIM, ESCHERSHEIM, ECKENHEIM, GINNHEIM, PREUNGESHEIM, SECKBACH, FECHENHEIM, BÜRGEL, OFFENBACH, OBERRAD, NIEDERRAD, GRIESHEIM, RÖDELHEIM, HAUSEN, PRAUNHEIM,

aux travailleurs étrangers qui se trouvent à Mannheim-Ludwigshafen et leur banlieue: SANDHOFEN, WALDHOF, KÄFERTAL, WALLSTADT, FEUDENHEIM, SECKENHEIM, NECKARAU, MUNDENHEIM, RHEINGÖNHEIM, MUTTERSTADT, FRIESENHEIM, OGGERSHEIM, OPPAU, EDESHEIM, FRANKENTAL.

**Travailleurs étrangers — vivez pour votre famille et votre patrie. Refusez de mourir travaillant pour l'Allemagne.**

**DWIGHT D. EISENHOWER**

**Général, Commandant Suprême, Forces Expeditionnaires Alliées**

Najwyższe dowództwo ...rzonych sił ekspedycyjnych

**DO ROBOTNIKÓW POLSKICH W OBREBIE FRANKFURTU NAD MENEM I LUDWIGSHAFEN**

NAJWYŻSZY Dowódzca dotychczas radził wam oraź innym cudzoziemskim robotnikom, abyście się nie dali ewakuować lecz poszukali sobie bezpieczną kryjówkę w pobliżu waszego miejsca pracy i tam czekali na przyjście wojsk aljanckich. Najwyższy Dowódzca niniejszym wydaje nową specjalną instrukcję przeznaczoną wyłącznie dla tych z was, którzy się znajdują w obrębie Frankfurtu nad Menem i Mannheim-Ludwigshafen

1) Przemysł wojenny zostanie całkowicie zniszczony. Znaczy to że obszar Frankfurtu nad Menem i Ludwigshafen stanie się pułapką śmierci.

2) Najwyższy Dowódzca poleca przeto wszystkim robotnikom cudzoziemskim na wyżej wymienionych obszarach natychmiast opuścić swe miejsca pracy i swe kwatery, schronić się w najbezpieczniejszym miejscu, jakie mogą znaleźć w najbliższej okolicy i pozostać tam aż bitwa minie.

3) Najwyższy Dowódzca podkreśla, że instrukcja niniejsza nie odnosi się do robotników cudzoziemskich na innych obszarach. Dotyczy ona wyłącznie robotników cudzoziemskich na obszarze miasta Frankfurt i' przedmieść Frankfurtu: NIEDERURSEL, HEDDERNHEIM, ESCHERSHEIM, ECKENHEIM, GINNHEIM, PREUNGESHEIM, SECKBACH, FECHENHEIM, BÜRGEL, OFFENBACH, OBERRAD, NIEDERRAD, GRIESHEIM, RÖDELHEIM, HAUSEN, PRAUNHEIM,

oraz robotników cudzoziemskich na obszarze miast Mannheim i Ludwigshafen i następujących przedmieść Mannheim-Ludwigshafen: SANDHOFEN, WALDHOF, KÄFERTAL, WALLSTADT, FEUDENHEIM, SECKENHEIM, NECKARAU, MUNDENHEIM, RHEINGÖNHEIM MUTTERSTADT, FRIESENHEIM, OGGERSHEIM, OPPAU, EDESHEIM, FRANKENTAL.

**Robotnicy cudzoziemscy — ratujcie życie dla rodziny i ojczyzny. Odmawiajcie umierać pracując w Niemczech.**

**DWIGHT D. EISENHOWER**

**General, Najwyższy Dowódzca Sprzymierzonych Sił Ekspedycyjnych.**

Provolání Nejvyššího Velitels... ...ojeneckých Expedičních Armád

**K ČESKOSLOVENSKÝM DĚLNÍKŮM PRACUJÍCÍM V OBLASTECH FRANKFURT AM MAIN A MANNHEIM-LUDWIGSHAFEN**

AŽ doposud Nejvyšší Velitel vám, jakož i jiným cizím dělníkům v západním Německu, radil, abyste se nenechali evakuovat, ale abyste si našli bezpečný útulek v blízkosti vašeho místa zaměstnání, a abyste tam vyčkali příchodu Spojeneckých Armád. Nejvyšší Velitel nyní vydává nové a zvláštní nařízení, které se týká vás, kteří jste v oblastech Frankfurt a Mannheim- Ludwigshafen.

1) Zbrojařský průmysl bude zničen. To znamená, že celá oblast Frankfurt a Mannheim-Ludwigshafen se stane pastí smrti.

2) Nejvyšší Velitel proto nařizuje všem cizím dělníkům v uvedených oblastech, aby ihned opustili svá místa zaměstnání a své ubikace, a uchýlili se do nejbezpečnějšího místa, které mohou najít v okolní krajině, a aby tam zůstali až se bitva přežene.

3) Nejvyšší Velitel zdůrazňuje, že toto nařízení se netýká cizích dělníků v jiných oblastech. Týká se pouze cizích dělníků ve Frankfurtu a jeho předměstích. NIEDERURSEL, HEDDERNHEIM, ESCHERSHEIM ECKENHEIM, GINNHEIM, PREUNGESHEIM, SECKBACH, FECHENHEIM, BÜRGEL, OFFENBACH, OBERRAD, NIEDERRAD, GRIESHEIM, RÖDELHEIM, HAUSEN, PRAUNHEIM,

jakož i cizích dělníků v Mannheim-Ludwigshafen a následujících předměstích: SANDHOFEN, WALDHOF, KÄFERTAL, WALLSTADT, FEUNDENHEIM, SECENHEIM, NECKARAU, MUNDENHEIM, RHEINGÖNHEIM, NECKARAU, MUNDENHEIM, RHEINGÖNHEIM, MUTTERSTADT, FRIESENHEIM, OGGERSHEIM, OPPAU, EDESHEIM, FRANKENTAL.

**Českoslovenští dělníci — udržte se na živu pro vaši rodinu a vlast. Odmítněte položit život při práci v Německu.**

**DWIGHT D. EISENHOWER**

**Generál, Nejvyšší Velitel Spojeneckých Expedičních Armád**

Comando Su... Inter-Alleato

**AI LAVORATORI ITALIANI NELLE ZONE DI FRANCOFORTE SUL MENO E DI MANNHEIM-LUDWIGSHAFEN**

IL Comandante Supremo ha, fino ad ora, consigliato a voi — come a tutti gli altri lavoratori stranieri che si trovano nella Germania occidentale, di opporvi allo sfollamento forzato, e di trovare un rifugio sicuro nelle vicinanze del vostro posto di lavoro e di aspettare lì le Armate Alleate Ora egli emana queste nuove istruzioni speciali che sono per quelli di voi che si trovano nelle zone di Francoforte sul Meno e Mannheim-Ludwigshafen

1) Le industrie belliche verranno distrutte. Questo significa che tutti coloro che si troveranno nelle zone di Francoforte sul Meno e Mannheim-Ludwigshafen saranno in pericolo di morte.

2) Il Comandante Supremo perciò dà istruzioni perchè tutti i lavoratori stranieri nei soprannominati distretti lascino immediatamente il loro lavoro e si allontanino dalle loro abitazioni e trovino rifugio nel più sicuro posto possibile nella campagna circostante, per restarvi fino a quando la battaglia sia passata.

3) Il Comandante Supremo mette in rilievo che queste istruzioni non sono destinate ai lavoratori stranieri delle altre zone Queste istruzioni sono esclusivamente per i lavoratori stranieri che si trovano a Francoforte e nei seguenti sobborghi di Francoforte. NIEDERURSEL, HEDDERNHEIM, ESCHERSHEIM, ECKENHEIM, GINNHEIM, PREUNGESHEIM, SECKBACH, FECHENHEIM, BÜRGEL, OFFENBACH, OBERRAD, NIEDERRAD, GRIESHEIM, RÖDELHEIM, HAUSEN, PRAUNHEIM.

ai lavoratori stranieri di Mannheim-Ludwigshafen e dei seguenti sobborghi di Mannheim-Ludwigshafen. SANDHOFEN, WALDHOF, KÄFERTAL, WALLSTADT, FEUDENHEIM, SECKENHEIM, NECKARAU, MUNDENHEIM, RHEINGÖNHEIM, MUTTERSTADT, FRIESENHEIM, OGGERSHEIM, OPPAU, EDESHEIM, FRANKENTAL.

**Lavoratori stranieri — tenetevi in vita per le vostre famiglie e per la vostra Patria. Rifiutatevi di morire lavorando per la Germania.**

**DWIGHT D. EISENHOWER**

**Generale, Comandante Supremo delle Forze Alleate di Spedizione**

## TO FRENCH WORKERS IN THE FRANKFURT AM MAIN AND MANNHEIM-LUDWIGSHAFEN AREAS

THE Supreme Commander, up till now, has advised you, along with all other foreign workers in Western Germany, not to permit yourself to be evacuated, but to find a safe refuge in the vicinity of your work and there to await the Allied Armies. He now issues a new special instruction which applies to those of you in Frankfurt and Mannheim-Ludwigshafen areas.

1) The armament industries will be destroyed. This means that the whole Frankfurt and Mannheim-Ludwigshafen areas will become death-traps.

2) The Supreme Commander therefore instructs all foreign workers in the above-named areas to leave their places of work and their billets immediately, to take refuge in the safest place they can find in the adjacent countryside, and to stay there until the battle has passed.

3) The supreme Commander emphasizes that these instructions do not apply to foreign workers in other areas, they are addressed only to foreign workers in Frankfurt and the suburbs of Frankfurt: NIEDERURSEL, HEDDERNHEIM, ESCHERSHEIM, ECKENHEIM, GINNHEIM, PREUNGESHEIM, SECKBACH, FECHENHEIM, BURGEL, OFFENBACH, OBERRAD, NIEDERRAD, GRIESEHEIM, RÖDELHEIM, HAUSEN, PRAUNHEIM.

To foreign workers in Mannheim and Ludwigshafen and the following suburbs of Mannheim and Ludwigshafen, SANDHOFEN, WALDHOF, KAFERTAL, WALLSTADT, FEUDENHEIM, SECKENHEIM, NECKARAU, MUNDENHEIM, RHEINGONHEIM, MUTTERSTADT, FRIESENHEIM, OGGERSHEIM, OPPAU, EDESHEIM, FRANKENTHAL.

Foreign workers — live for your family and country. Refuse to die working in Germany.

Dwight D. Eisenhower
DWIGHT D. EISENHOWER,
Supreme Commander Allied Expeditionary Force.

## TO POLISH WORKERS IN THE FRANKFURT AM MAIN AND MANNHEIM-LUDWIGSHAFEN AREAS

THE Supreme Commander, up till now, has advised you, along with all other foreign workers in Western Germany, not to permit yourself to be evacuated, but to find a safe refuge in the vicinity of your work and there to await the Allied Armies. He now issues a new special instruction which applies to those of you in Frankfurt and Mannheim-Ludwigshafen areas.

1) The armament industries will be destroyed. This means that the whole Frankfurt and Mannheim-Ludwigshafen areas will become death-traps.

2) The Supreme Commander therefore instructs all foreign workers in the above-named areas to leave their places of work and their billets immediately, to take refuge in the safest place they can find in the adjacent countryside, and to stay there until the battle has passed.

3) The supreme Commander emphasizes that these instructions do not apply to foreign workers in other areas, they are addressed only to foreign workers in Frankfurt and the suburbs of Frankfurt: NIEDERURSEL, HEDDERNHEIM, ESCHERSHEIM, ECKENHEIM, GINNHEIM, PREUNGESHEIM, SECKBACH, FECHENHEIM, BURGEL, OFFENBACH, OBERRAD, NIEDERRAD, GRIESEHEIM, RÖDELHEIM, HAUSEN, PRAUNHEIM.

To foreign workers in Mannheim and Ludwigshafen and the following suburbs of Mannheim and Ludwigshafen, SANDHOFEN, WALDHOF, KAFERTAL, WALLSTADT, FEUDENHEIM, SECKENHEIM, NECKARAU, MUNDENHEIM, RHEINGONHEIM, MUTTERSTADT, FRIESENHEIM, OGGERSHEIM, OPPAU, EDESHEIM, FRANKENTHAL.

Foreign workers — live for your family and country. Refuse to die working in Germany.

Dwight D. Eisenhower
DWIGHT D. EISENHOWER,
Supreme Commander Allied Expeditionary Force

## TO CZECHOSLOVAK WORKERS IN THE FRANKFURT AM MAIN AND MANNHEIM-LUDWIGSHAFEN AREAS

THE Supreme Commander, up till now, has advised you, along with all other foreign workers in Western Germany, not to permit yourself to be evacuated, but to find a safe refuge in the vicinity of your work and there to await the Allied Armies. He now issues a new special instruction which applies to those of you in Frankfurt and Mannheim-Ludwigshafen areas.

1) The armament industries will be destroyed. This means that the whole Frankfurt and Mannheim-Ludwigshafen areas will become death-traps.

2) The Supreme Commander therefore instructs all foreign workers in the above-named areas to leave their places of work and their billets immediately, to take refuge in the safest place they can find in the adjacent countryside, and to stay there until the battle has passed.

3) The supreme Commander emphasizes that these instructions do not apply to foreign workers in other areas, they are addressed only to foreign workers in Frankfurt and the suburbs of Frankfurt: NIEDERURSEL, HEDDERNHEIM, ESCHERSHEIM, ECKENHEIM, GINNHEIM, PREUNGESHEIM, SECKBACH, FECHENHEIM, BURGEL, OFFENBACH, OBERRAD, NIEDERRAD, GRIESEHEIM, RÖDELHEIM, HAUSEN, PRAUNHEIM.

To foreign workers in Mannheim and Ludwigshafen and the following suburbs of Mannheim and Ludwigshafen, SANDHOFEN, WALDHOF, KAFERTAL, WALLSTADT, FEUDENHEIM, SECKENHEIM, NECKARAU, MUNDENHEIM, RHEINGONHEIM, MUTTERSTADT, FRIESENHEIM, OGGERSHEIM, OPPAU, EDESHEIM, FRANKENTHAL.

Foreign workers — live for your family and country. Refuse to die working in Germany.

Dwight D. Eisenhower
DWIGHT D. EISENHOWER,
Supreme Commander Allied Expeditionary Force.

## TO ITALIAN WORKERS IN THE FRANKFURT AM MAIN AND MANNHEIM-LUDWIGSHAFEN AREAS

THE Supreme Commander, up till now, has advised you, along with all other foreign workers in Western Germany, not to permit yourself to be evacuated, but to find a safe refuge in the vicinity of your work and there to await the Allied Armies. He now issues a new special instruction which applies to those of you in Frankfurt and Mannheim-Ludwigshafen areas.

1) The armament industries will be destroyed. This means that the whole Frankfurt and Mannheim-Ludwigshafen areas will become death-traps.

2) The Supreme Commander therefore instructs all foreign workers in the above-named areas to leave their places of work and their billets immediately, to take refuge in the safest place they can find in the adjacent countryside, and to stay there until the battle has passed.

3) The supreme Commander emphasizes that these instructions do not apply to foreign workers in other areas, they are addressed only to foreign workers in Frankfurt and the suburbs of Frankfurt: NIEDERURSEL, HEDDERNHEIM, ESCHERSHEIM, ECKENHEIM, GINNHEIM, PREUNGESHEIM, SECKBACH, FECHENHEIM, BURGEL, OFFENBACH, OBERRAD, NIEDERRAD, GRIESEHEIM, RÖDELHEIM, HAUSEN, PRAUNHEIM.

To foreign workers in Mannheim and Ludwigshafen and the following suburbs of Mannheim and Ludwigshafen, SANDHOFEN, WALDHOF, KAFERTAL, WALLSTADT, FEUDENHEIM, SECKENHEIM, NECKARAU, MUNDENHEIM, RHEINGONHEIM, MUTTERSTADT, FRIESENHEIM, OGGERSHEIM, OPPAU, EDESHEIM, FRANKENTHAL.

Foreign workers — live for your family and country. Refuse to die working in Germany.

Dwight D. Eisenhower
DWIGHT D. EISENHOWER,
Supreme Commander Allied Expeditionary Force.

further sobering agent to those who still believe that America can live in a world unto itself.

And General of the Army George C. Marshall in his war-end report on October 10, 1945 wrapped it up this way:

". . . . For probably the last time in the history of warfare . . . ocean distances were a vital factor in our defense. We may elect again to depend on others and the whim of error of potential enemies, but if we do we will be carrying the treasure and freedom of this great Nation in a paper bag. . . ."

Because propaganda is a grim, realistic business our enemies made full use of its facilities together with all the distortions, the lies, the hates, the eye-wash and the hogwash which went into making out a case for their side.

In sharp contrast, American propaganda specialized exclusively in the truth, concentrating on news as its principal ammunition. Come low water (December 1941 to January 1943), or high water (February 1943 to May 1945), we never slipped in telling the truth. We omitted, but we never lied. Critics of our omissions never understood the America's propaganda agency—the Office of War Information—was not in the business of giving our enemies entertainment or even a free news service. Both the Office of War Information and the military and naval Psychological Warfare branched which OWI serviced with material and personnel, were strictly in the business of using propaganda as a weapon of warfare. We did not carry the torch for democracy. Our only interest was winning the war.

American psychological warfare teams gave the German troops and civilians the fastest and most accurate news service possible. On the American Fifth Army sector of the Italian front, German troops received the news of the Russian encirclement of East Prussia within an hour after the news was announced in Moscow. Several hundred surrenders resulted among Germans from East Prussia, proving that when it hits its target news as a weapon of war as potent as a flame thrower.

While we got into the propaganda business because we had to, our enemies have made it a war-to-war "must." Since we now are well aware that wars do not start with shooting but actually begin with words and ideas many years before, it should be no particular surprise to learn that World War II began immediately at the formal end to the shooting of World War I in 1918.

The German Army was beaten in 1918, but the German General Staff was not. The German generals shed the blame, conveniently placing it on the "breakdown of German civilian morale." The alibi stuck and soon was repeated often enough—as with any lie—so that all Germans and most of the world believed it.

Field Marshal Wilhelm Keitel, German Chief of Staff, has joined scores of other Nazi bigwigs in trying to shed the blame of 1933-1945. During his testimony at the Nuremberg trials, Keitel called himself just "a liveried lackey of Hitler." The tune has been the same from all other defendants. Dr. Hans Heinrich Lammers, former chief of the German Chancellery, insisted that Hitler was the German Government.

Listen to the words of one member of the German General Staff, General Bernhardi, who, immediately after the Armistice of 1918, said:

"We need a respite. The peaceful declarations of our government are welcome. It is better not to hint at the coming war."

What General Bernhardi said is no different from what a well-educated, intelligent German lieutenant of the Wehrmacht engineers and an American prisoner of war, said in March 1945 in a U. S. Army hospital in Naples about seven weeks before the German unconditional surrender:

"This horrible slaughter! Why does the High Command allow the slaughter of fine German young men? We need them for the next war!"

To carry on their war without actually firing guns—which they didn't have—was no great problem to the German General Staff beginning in 1919. Finding a sleep potion to be administered to the rest of the world, was simple. This is how it was done.

After the last war—and now after this one too—the people of the world were war weary. They wanted peace. This was particularly true of the democratic countries like ours. We have always loathed war and always will. This played right into the hands of the German General Staff, whose business was war and who have convinced the German people that Germany's destiny is war and world conquest—then, now and a hundred years from now.

The German Government mouthed one peaceful declaration after another. A vast number of German anti-war books appeared, which gave the democracies the idea that the last thing any German wanted was war. Undoubtedly the men who wrote the books were really opposed to war, but whether they were or were not, they certainly played into the hands of the German High Command.

German war veterans' organizations echoed the theme. Some of the veterans believed it. When Hitler came to power in 1933 he exploited this well planted fallacy for all it was worth—and it was worth plenty. From 1933 to 1941 he gave the world as expert a lesson in double talk as history has ever recorded. While he talked peace out of the right side of his mouth, he was giving orders for the military invasion of Czechoslovakia, Austria, Poland, Russia, France, Denmark, Norway, etc. from the left side. This we-don't-want-war theme was just one in the German medicine bag to lull the world into a deep sleep. An added sleep potion was the wail and cry of the "inequities" of the Versailles treaty.

The Germans stopped at nothing to develop propaganda. They even deliberately ruined their country with inflation as part of the plan to seek the sympathy of the world. And didn't we feel sorry for the "poor underdog" Germans, as Americans feel sorry for any underdog!

The organized inflation prompted Karl Helferich to say:

"Let them (the German people) suffer a little longer. When they feel the full brunt of inflation, they will start hating. And we shall see to it that their hatred is concentrated on the Republic, on the Jews, and on foreigners."

Further evidence of how the German General Staff first made "mark fodder" and then "cannon fodder" later, came from State Secretary for the Reichsbank

Brinkmann, who proudly told American business men how thrilling it was to smuggle currency in and out of Germany as part of the inflation scheme.

The inflation had a double propaganda edge: (1) By wiping out the savings of the lower and middle classes their faith in the republic was destroyed, and (2) to the rest of the world the German appeared as the poor, abused, penniless underdog.

The mere formality of an end to the actual shooting is no reason for Germans to stop the war. As recently as July 18, 1945, two-and-a-half months after their unconditional surrender, the Germans were still fighting the war against the Allies inside Germany with rumors. The objective: to generate hatred against and among the Allies in an attempt to rid themselves of "foreign domination." They will never stop until their ultimate objective is achieved. And if killing American occupation troops will do the trick, they'll do that too.

To this day few Germans, if any, will admit they lost the war. Among themselves this is simply an unpleasant interlude during which they will bide their time, then lay the groundwork for the next phase of the shooting, or World War III.

The German loss of World War I was blamed accurately on the Allies, but for reasons different from the real ones. The German World War I misery was blamed on the Allied blockade. As usual, the Germans neglected to mention the U-boat blockade they attempted and failed to impose against the Allies. A "mere omission," but a powerful argument for an underdog groping for an excuse—even a phony one.

To the average American soldier now on occupation duty in Germany, the average German is just a "kraut." During the heat of combat, the term "kraut" expressed everything the GI hated in the German—his brutality, his sneakiness, his shooting of American medics through the center of the red cross decorating the medics' helmets; his shooting in cold blood of captured American soldiers; his unspeakable acts of savagery committed in the concentration camps. "Kraut" was a term of hate.

More than a year has passed; the word "kraut" now has become an unemotional identification of the average German. Slowly it is developing into a friendly term referring to the German seen walking to work or to the Military Government offices every day. Most American soldiers during their occupation duties see only Germans day in and day out. They see only German women, most of whom have lost their men. The frauleins are only too willing to act "friendly" to American soldiers, who are a source of physiological comfort, extra food and a plentiful supply of American cigarettes and candy.

The GI's see the Germans well dressed. He never bothers to think they are wearing the loot of Europe, including the clothes of German gas chamber victims. They appear well fed. But the GI has forgotten that for years the Germans lived on the stolen food of Europe and at the expense of millions of starved bodies. He finds the Germans polite. The soldier does not pause to think that the Germans have strong motives: ingratiating themselves with occupation troops for extra favors now and for lulling the troops into a false sense of security. The "krauts" are biding their time.

If we fail to tell our occupation troops that underneath the false German front are deep, evil roots, we will have fought and won an empty victory. Behind the smiles and honeyed words—even of the bedroom variety—are the enemies responsible for the deaths of more than 25,000,000 human beings.

Today, most Germans meet an American soldier in Germany with their hat in hand. Some even talk to Americans with their hands in their pockets, a German gesture of contempt. But that may not be for long. Soon under the hat and in the pocket will be a gun or a knife. There will be honeyed words drooling from innocent-looking German mouths, but behind the backs of Americans the propaganda campaign of hate against Americans will outdo the campaign of hate during the 1919 occupation which was as vicious as any mind could conceive.

The year 1919 is being repeated today. The Germans don't like the idea of an occupation army on their soil. Of course, it was all right for Germans to occupy most of Europe between 1939 to 1945. But that was different. The occupiers were Germans. To attempt to reconcile the German mind or argue with it is a waste of time. It is safer to go on the assumption that their every act, their every word, has an ulterior motive which bodes no good for any American and for the rest of the world.

In 1919 and 1920 the Germans slandered the Americans to the British and the British to the Americans. Today, it is the Russians to the British, the Americans to the Russians, and so on and on and on. The "divide and conquer" theory, used so successfully by the Germans while they were winning, hasn't and won't change. It is being used with deadly accuracy at every opportunity.

Recently, Ernest Hauser, foreign roving correspondent for *The Saturday Evening Post,* indicated how deeply is rooted the "carry-on-the-propaganda" theme within the German mind, when he wrote:

"The average German today says: 'The only hope of Germany's salvation is a war between America and Russia'."

Attempting to drive a wedge among the Allies was one of Germany's greatest objectives before and during World War II.

Germany today is simply living up to the plans carefully laid down by its braintrusters such as Professor Banse, whose staggering book, published in the United States in 1934 under the title *Germany Prepares for War* stated this conclusion:

"In war and in peace, the higher command must always treat the psychological as the most important factor—along with arms, equipment and training—in their plans and calculations. This applies equally to one's own troops and the enemy's."

Banse was thorough. He laid down an outline for planning war as follows:

"Good propaganda should begin in peace-time and operate in such a way that the country running it reaps its fruits as soon as war is declared. War-time propaganda ought to be merely the more concentrated and, of course, more vigorous continuation of peace-time propaganda . . .

"In detail the things to be done are: setting up centers in foreign capitals; literary propaganda, by influencing the press and also by producing books and pamphlets; getting up effective films and broadcasting items; putting up public-utility buildings adapted to the character of the people; i. e., reading-rooms or drinking fountains or industrial institutes, as the case may be; finally mouth-to-mouth propaganda *with the help of native agents.*"

That is exactly what the Nazis did from 1933 to 1941.

# VI
# GERMANY IN AMERICA

The story of Germany in America is not one of which we should be particularly proud. The Germans almost took our country away from us—and right from under our very noses.

Only now after we have decisively trounced Germany on the battlefield and blasted Japan into surrender is the story fully revealed of how close we came to losing before we got started. What is even more sickening is the full realization of the help the Germans received from people who called themselves Americans. These were not Americans of German extraction, but native-born Americans who fell for the Nazi sales talk and then proceeded to spread the poison on their own.

The damage these American stooges wrought is no different from the damage they might have done had they been Nazi saboteurs, paid to destroy our war plants, and military installations, and kill our citizens.

Before and during World War I, Germany concentrated on actual physical sabotage within the United States. They blew up ammunition dumps (the Black Tom disaster); they destroyed military equipment (the

Kingsland disaster); they wrecked more than 40 industrial plants and freight yards and at least 47 American ships were sunk by fire bombs planted before they sailed from American ports. In all, they cost hundreds of American lives and $150,000,000 damage to essential war resources.

The German method in World War II—before and during the shooting—was very different. Because we had a Federal Bureau of Investigation, which was almost infallible, the Germans concentrated on psychological sabotage, which we know now is as effective as physical sabotage.

Before a single American soldier was killed or wounded on a battlefield in combat with the enemy, many millions of American civilians had already become casualties from the enemy's war of words and ideas.

German psychological saboteurs and their American stooges had five major objectives:

1. To disrupt and disunite the American people by stirring up race hatred, religious hatred and antagonism among opposing groups.
2. To undermine the confidence of the American people in their form of government, with heavy emphasis on discrediting the administration of President Roosevelt.
3. To isolate the United States physically and psychologically and thus prevent it from joining an anti-Axis alliance and prevent it from aiding nations attacked by the Axis.

4. To prevent the United States from being prepared for its inevitable participation in World War II.
5. To build a Fascist party in America, preferably one bedecked in American colors and patriotic-sounding slogans, which would act as a fifth column ally to the Axis.

The Germans spent as much as $625,000,000 a year attempting to put this plan into action.

If the plan sounds fantastic, it is exactly what the Germans intended. While we Americans naively insisted "it's impossible," "it can't happen here," and "they wouldn't dare," the Germans and their stooges went right along doing exactly what we thought they wouldn't dare.

When we said the Germans wouldn't dare, we were indulging in wishful thinking. We hadn't learned, even after the 1940 era of wishful thinking, when Germany beat France and we hoped it wasn't true. Germany did beat France and we still thought within the mold into which the Nazis skillfully poured our minds.

While the F. B. I. guarded the sabotage front so that not a single case of enemy-inspired sabotage was committed before or during the war, we left the gates wide open for the German psychological saboteurs to operate. They roamed our country as though they owned it, carrying on open warfare with honeyed words which they carefully wrapped in red, white and blue bunting. What they said through their American stooges sounded patriotic, but it really was shooting us in the back.

Huey Long once said that if Fascism ever came to America, it would be on a program of "Americanism."

The Germans sent their stooges over by the thousands—soldiers without uniform, but soldiers nevertheless—who could wage war by working their "divide-and-conquer" technique within the United States.

These agents came well armed with information about us, more information than we knew about ourselves. The findings about America had been compiled from German agents who had operated without interference in the United States since the end of World War I. All the information they gathered in the U.S.A. and every scrap of information about us from indirect sources, such as newspapers, magazines and books, was carefully sifted and analyzed in the special German psychological warfare laboratory which had been established by the German General Staff at No. 58 Lehrterstrasse, Berlin, in 1929, fully three years before Hitler came to power.

The primary interest of the laboratory was to find America's "trouble center." Once determined, this trouble center was to be used as a basis for all propaganda against the United States.

The trouble center in the United States, the German laboratory experts decided, was the political fight between the pro-New Deal and anti-New Deal forces. Since the political party in power offered neither aid, comfort or hope to the Nazis, their cue was obviously to attack the Roosevelt administration. The overwhelming majority of the opposition to President Roosevelt, of course, had nothing in common with the Nazis or their American stooges. In fact, "support" from the Nazis and their American sympathizers proved embarrassing to the anti-Roosevelt forces, particularly when the Nazis had a kind word to say for the opposition during German broadcasts to the United States.

In 1935, orders were issued to Nazi agents in the United States to concentrate on fomenting antagonism against President Roosevelt and his administration and to spread propaganda that the "government of the United States had fallen into the hands of Jews and Communists."

Amazingly enough, the campaign, based on a fantastic falsehood, was believed by too many Americans. The Nazis had pushed the right hate button.

Anti-Semitism was nothing new to the Germans. They had used it successfully throughout Europe. The Nazi mark of anti-Semitism is stamped today all over Europe and in many places where it had never existed before. It has left its mark in the United States where they found the poison of anti-Semitism the best weapon possible.

Every single Naz and Nazi-American stooge was and is a professional or amateur anti-Semite.

No less an authority than Hitler's first press chief, Adolph-Viktor von Koerber, had this to say on the subject of anti-Semitism:

"It furnishes an excellent international vehicle. There is a certain measure of anti-Semitism in almost every country in the world. By assuming leadership over the anti-Semitic movement, Hitler intended to get his finger into every national pie throughout the world. And he was right!"

Hitler's work in America was based on his familiar theme, "Let the enemy defeat himself." He wanted Americans to do his dirty work here and he succeeded in getting it done. He even used traitorous Americans like Jane Anderson, Fred Kaltenbach, Ezra Pound and Otto Koischwitz for his broadcasts from Germany.

Working with Hitler's American stooges were some of the so-called German-American organizations. The "American" part of these hyphenated groups was a sham. All operated on Hitler's basic principle, "Once a German always a German."

The Germans had not forgotten what one of their scholarly torch-bearers had written in 1903:

"Germany's great enemy in the 20th century will be the United States."

While Germany hoped to win the war against America with words, there were some hot-headed Nazis who became impatient in 1937 and made frank statements to the press in New York. One was Hermann Schwartzmann, a beefy, slow-witted baker, who held a high position in the German-American Bund, the adjunct of the Nazi Party in the United States. Schwartzmann warned:

"Blood will flow in the streets of America!"

He wasn't talking idly because in a Federal Court action in New York in 1942 to denaturalize 26 of these Nazis who had taken out American citizenship—with their fingers crossed—one of the former comrades testified that the belts these German-American Bundsmen Storm Troopers wore were especially made for use as a whip which could slash an adversary's face to ribbons.

Nazi organizations, made up almost exclusively of Americans of former German nationality, fell flat on their faces in an attempt to stir up anything except contempt. While they did inject some poison, the lion's share of the task assigned them by Hitler was achieved by Americans who did his work in America as respectable fronts. Between 1933 and 1939, scores of organizations sprang up in the United States and peddled the Hitler line.

They called themselves "American Crusaders," "American Silver Shirts," "The Christian Front," "Protestant War Veterans of America" and any other sweet, patriotic-sounding name which would disarm the average American who believed implicitly in labels.

A man with a goatee on his face and Nazism on his brain, William Dudly Pelley, was one of Hitler's many busy bees in America. He was finally convicted of sedition. Charles E. Coughlin's *Social Justice* was banned by the United States Post Office Department as "clearly seditious."

Once Coughlin published an article in his *Social Justice* which he signed with his name. Marquis Childs, Washington correspondent for the *St. Louis Post Dispatch,* discovered that this article was word for word, comma for comma, period for period, a speech made by Dr. Goebbels over the German domestic radio. Coughlin called it "a coincidence."

Many of these organizations took their themes and the material for their publications directly from Germany—from the *Welt-Dienst.* This was the German news service agency set up primarily to furnish Nazi-angled material for foreign consumption.

*Welt-Dienst's* poison was distributed in 19 different languages throughout the world, but lots of the poison was concentrated within the United States,

Unwittingly and in good faith—in keeping with its international postal agreements—the U. S. Post

Office distributed the Nazi propaganda free within the United States. (Since the Nazi propaganda was German government material, all the Nazis had to do was print stamps and paste them on their propaganda packages. The U.S. Post Office delivered them on a reciprocity basis, assuming that if any American wished to send pro-democratic material to Germany he could.)

Nazi brazenness in their attempt to defeat America through words and ideas knew no bounds. Hard as it is to believe, the Nazis concocted and successfully carried out a plot to use the *Congressional Record,* official publication of the Congress of the United States, as a Nazi propaganda transmission belt.

They even went one impertinent step further: they imposed on unsuspecting Congressmen and used their franking privilege to mail the poison throughout the United States. The brains of this plot was George Sylvester Viereck, a German propagandist in World War I and a paid Nazi apologist from 1933 to 1941.

The Germans organized a chain of phony, respectable front organizations, such as one called "The American Fellowship Forum." It was run by a man named Dr. Friedrich Auhagen. He denied he was a German agent until newspaper exposés sent him fleeing to San Francisco where he was arrested just as he boarded a Japanese boat bound for Yokahama. He was convicted later of failing to register as an agent of a foreign government.

German stooges jumped with both feet and money into movements such as the "America First Committee," and the "No Foreign Wars Committee," both highly praised by the German short-wave radio in its broadcasts to the United States.

The *Chicago Tribune,* and the *New York Daily News,* two of the leading isolationist, the Germans-can't-harm-us newspapers in the United States, became the most quoted American newspapers over the Nazi short-wave radio.

The Nazis made a big splash of one *Chicago Tribune* quote which stated:

"It is absurd to think that the Germans want to go to war with us."

Lindbergh, who had won America's heart as an aviation hero, went on the stump to repeat the Nazi line, although he proclaimed himself as 100 percent American. He told a nation-wide radio audience in September, 1941:

"The three greatest advocates of war in this country are the British, the Jews, and President Roosevelt."

It is identical with what the German short-wave radio had been saying for two years and what every last Nazi stooge had been repeating.

In January, 1944, 30 Americans, many of them native Americans, were indicted by a Federal Grand Jury on charges of conspiring with "the Nazi Party to accomplish the objectives of said Nazi Party in the United States."

These objectives, according to the indictment, included undermining and impairing "the loyalty and morale of the military and naval forces of the United States." The case ended in a mistrial with the death of the presiding judge. The question of retrying the thirty under a new indictment is now pending.

The Germans financed their own publishing house in the United States. Flanders Hall, with headquarters in New Jersey, published scores of books which were anti-American, anti-Semitic, anti-British, and all Nazi-inspired.

All these activities attempted to achieve one objective: to strengthen and replenish Germany while keeping America out of war.

The height of the Nazi attempt to create confusion, discord and divide America into two huge hating camps was reached in 1940 and 1941, during the "great debate:" intervention versus isolation.

We have learned by bitter experience that we can remain about as isolated in the world as the man who goes to Coney Island on a hot Sunday afternoon in July. But the Germans almost sold us a bill of goods by jumping into the "great debate" with money and lies, confusing thousands of well-meaning Americans.

America was shocked out of its sleep and temporary blindness which the Nazis had imposed on us, when the Japs attacked Pearl Harbor. By that time we had been as badly disarmed psychologically as France had been in 1939 and 1940.

It was a close shave—closer than most intelligent Americans like to remember—but we grabbed our six-shooters just in the nick of time.

But German propaganda has been so strong, that it has spilled over into other countries, leaving its mark throughout the world. It can be called "Hitler's legacy," because although the Germans are a defeated nation and Hitler is dead, his poison lingers on, threatening to infect the world again.

In Holland, the most pressing domestic problem is not reconstruction, but anti-Semitism. In Argentina, the Nazi pattern is being followed successfully with the Fascist mass appeal. In Spain, Fascism based on Nazi ideology remains intact. In the United States, the Fascist-minded rabble-rousers, dormant during the war, are active again.

The nationalist groups hiding behind a red, white and blue bunting are ranting throughout the United States, appealing to labor baiters, Jew baiters, Roosevelt-haters and Red-baiters by blaming World War II on Roosevelt and the Jews, mouthing the pre-Pearl Harbor words of the Nazis.

Demagogues, who were playing Hitler's game before December 7, 1941, are exploring the field of 12,000,000 American veterans. They will attempt to capitalize on the uneasiness and the resentment of the ex-GIs. Those who were in combat will not easily forget the hundreds of Nazi-written leaflets fired at them. The enemy "paper bullets" told them what America's Jew-baiters are telling them today.

In the south, the Ku Klux Klan, appealing to the Nazi-type of racial hokum, is carrying on violent anti-Negro propaganda "to keep the nigger in his place." But the Klan, not unmindful of Hitler's success with anti-Semitism, is using that theme too.

All of which adds up to the fact that America has not yet learned its lesson. Americans are still listening to enemies of democracy who use scapegoatism as a weapon of psychological warfare against the unsuspecting, victory-lulled people of the United States.

Those who thought that Nazism and its American stooge—the German-American Bund, died with the defeat of Germany, are in for a shock. Far from dead, the Nazi microbes among the Bundists are as virulent as ever. Today, they are parading under the respectable mantle of "relief societies"—relief for Germany at a time when the Germans have an obligation to all of Europe and all of Europe needs relief.

The time for relief to Germany may come after Germany's victims are cared for. But the Bundist "reliefers" are appealing now to the traditional kindliness of Americans. Behind this appeal is the same cunning which contrived the Bund use of George Washington as a front for their phony Americanism. Germany's defeat has not dimmed the ardor of the Bund eager beavers. They are as shrewd and as conniving as ever. They are acting as apologists for "an honorably defeated Germany" while denouncing the United States and the United Nations for scuttling the rehabilitations of Germany. It is sheer impertinence, but what's a little impertinence among a people who are historically impertinent?

# VII
# GERMANY IN LATIN AMERICA

While the Germans were busy operating throughout Europe and the United. States, they decidedly had not neglected South America which, to them, had always been the great stepping-stone to North America.

Hundreds of millions of dollars in German money is invested in South American industry. Self-supporting branches of the huge German cartels, like I. G. Farben, the chemical trust, are deeply entrenched in South American economic life. The huge investment of German capital in South America, particularly in Argentina, is no accident. Again, it is part of the all-embracing plan for German world conquest.

The German plan to penetrate into South America was drawn up many years before Hitler took power. This plan for world domination had a triple "1A" priority, even when Hitler was just a stumble-bum in Austria. The idea of the plan is that it is supposed to work for Germany even in defeat. It is aimed at the eventual conquest of the United States, which the Germans know they must achieve before they can realize world domination.

Immediately after the close of World War I, German infiltration of Latin American countries by economic, political and military agents began. Captain Ernst Roehm, who organized the Nazi Storm Troopers for Hitler in 1934, was in Bolivia in 1925 as an adviser to the Bolivian Army. A prominent German aviator named Hammer turned up in Colombia as a representative of German aviation companies. His real mission was espionage and economic infiltration.

A German general became head of the Military Academy at San Salvador. Two other German generals became active in Chile, Paraguay and Peru, where they spread hatred of the United States, particularly among the officer corps.

Directing all this activity for the Germans was General Wilhelm von Faupel. He has not paused from his mission by such a "temporary" reverse as Germany's unconditional surrender. When he received his assignment from the German High Command, the plan was based on victory as well as defeat. His task now, as before, is to prepare the ground in South America for World War III, because in that war the Germans want the United States to fight in the Western Hemisphere.

As with most everything the Germans do, von Faupel's plan was nothing new in the world of German international conniving and chiseling. The establishment of a strong German influence over all of South America has been an old dream of the German General Staff. As far back as 1904, Ernest Hasse wrote:

"The Argentine and Brazilian republics and all other seedy South American states will accept our advice and listen to reason, voluntarily or under coercion. In 100 years, both South and North America will be conquered by the German *geist* (spirit or ideology) and the German Emperor will perhaps transfer his residence to New York."

Germans have carefully "colonized" throughout South America. The last authoritative estimate was that more than three million Germans had infiltrated into the southern continent, bringing with them the desire for world conquest and German "kultur," including all that both imply.

Argentina played a very important role in Joseph Goebbels' propaganda for Nazi Germany. A good idea of how the wind blew from Germany toward South America was this statement from Goebbels' "wind factory:"

"Argentina will one day be at the head of a tariff union comprising the nations in the southern half of South America. Such a focus of opposition against the United States will spread northward to place the dollar economy of Brazil in a difficult position."

That is economic warfare tied firmly to the tail of psychological warfare.

The wind that blew from Germany gathered strength within Argentina, where that country's Colonel Juan Peron let go with this one in June, 1944:

"In South America it is our mission to make the leadership of Argentina not only possible but indisputable. Hitler's fight in peace and war will guide us, Alliances will be the next step. We will get Bolivia and Chile, then it will be easy to exert pressure on Uruguay. These five nations will attract Brazil, due to its type of government and its important group of

Germans. Once Brazil has fallen, the South American continent will be ours. Following the German example, we will inculcate the masses with the necessary militarism."

It goes in here and it comes out there!

Regardless of Peron, the Latin American Nazi is positive that he can win in the coming election. If he does, Nazi money and Nazi political know-how will do the trick, even in a "free" election.

Basically, the tune in Latin America is the same except that more soft soap has been inserted into the tuba. When it comes out now, even after our victories in Europe and the Pacific, the result is much the same. Certainly, the United States won the war, but a few carbon copies of Hitler continue to rattle around in South America.

# VIII
# THE JAPANESE AND PROPAGANDA

The Japanese used propaganda as a double-barreled weapon. They attacked the hearts and minds of more than 300 million natives whom they wanted to enlist in their Greater East Asia Co-Prosperity Sphere, and they went after us—not to win us over but to neutralize us while they ran amuck through the Central and South Pacific and Southeast Asia.

Japanese propaganda was meshed to the German Psychological warfare plan up to a certain point. That point was one dictated by the Germans. If what the Japanese did fitted into German plans, well and good. If it didn't, the German propaganda chiefs in Japan decided the issue.

The Germans had a branch factory of their propaganda ministry in Japan. When the British blockade in the Atlantic made it unfeasible to attempt to get Nazi propaganda into the United States, it was radioed to Tokyo and printed on Japanese presses. Until November, 1941, German propaganda material prepared by the *Welt-Dienst* entered the United States from Japanese ships.

We know now that the Axis partners had no overall plan of military strategy. But we do know that there was definite collaboration on the psychological warfare strategy between the German and Jap ends of the Axis.

The Japanese propaganda warfare before the attack on Pearl Harbor was identical in pattern with that of the Germans. The only differences were the names, the places and the German appointment of their Japanese soul-mates as "honorary aryans." The parallel between the German propaganda themes and the Japanese is amazing. Here are a few of more than a score of deadly parallels:

| GERMANS | JAPANESE |
|---|---|
| *Fuehrer God*—Hitler as a God, loyalty to him highest virtue, justifying all crimes. | *Emperor-God*—Loyalty to Hirohito highest virtue, justifying all crimes. |
| *Lives pledged to Hitler*—Highest reward was to die for the Fuehrer. | *Lives pledged to Hirohito*—Highest reward was to die for the Emperor. |
| *Scapegoats*—Jews, Catholics, Protestants and Masons | *Scapegoats*—"Red-haired barbarians of the west" (British and Americans). |
| *Herrenvolk*—Super-race. | *Sons of Heaven*—Super-race. |
| *Plan of conquest*—One country at a time. | *Plan of conquest*—One country at a time. |
| *Quislings.* | *Puppet Governments.* |
| *Spain*—Used as proving ground for war. | *Manchuria*—Used as proving ground for war. |
| *New Order in Europe*—German destiny to rule the world. | *Hakko Ichiu*—"To bring the 8 corners of the world under one roof." |

As further proof that what the Germans did in their aggression was nothing new under the sun, witness the cooing of peace which came from the two fat, hissing doves the Japs sent to Washington at the moment a Japanese task force had sailed from Japan to attack Pearl Harbor.

The Japs' big propaganda theme before Pearl Harbor was her "peaceful intentions." It fooled a lot of people in the United States including many who should have known better, despite warnings by all American news correspondents in Japan who correctly predicted that no matter how we appeased Japan, she was sure to attack us sooner or later.

Joseph Newman, Tokyo correspondent for the *New York Herald Tribune,* telephoned a story to his paper in March 1941, stating flatly that Japan planned to attack us at Pearl Harbor before the year was out.

Japanese "peaceful intentions" included attacking Manchuria, China and blasting away at the morale of natives in Asia and the mandated Pacific Islands. We were pictured as the natives' worst enemies, the Japs as their best friends. The racial conflict of white vs. yellow was posed. We had no antidote for this poison because we had no official U. S. government information agency.

The Japanese avoided the truth like the bubonic plague then, just as they do now, except under orders from General MacArthur. Their people still don't know the real extent of Japanese defeat.

In the fall of 1941, at a time when Japanese spokesmen bemoaned that the United States refused to understand her "peaceful intentions," an American newspaper correspondent asked the Japanese Foreign

Office for some facts with which he could enlighten the American people about Japanese intentions.

The reply has a familiar ring to those of us who clearly see the pattern of our enemies. Here it is:

"Facts! Facts! Americans are interested in facts, whereas we know facts are of no importance. What is important is intuition."

The Japanese propaganda did not have the extensive network in the United States which the Germans had organized. The Jap equivalent of the German Ministry of Propaganda, the Board of Information, assumed correctly that with the exception of Americans living in Hawaii and the West Coast, the average American felt that Japan and Southeast Asia were too far away to cause any worry.

That was another one of our national errors because we are too prone to brush off as inconsequential anything that we do not fully understand.

Actually, the Japanese worked busily and diligently in the United States, concentrating principally on our large centers of population. There was the *Japanese-American Review* which dwelt on the wonders a tourist would behold in Japan. Propaganda references were subtly included with reports of how well the Japanese were getting along in Asia with the natives.

American newspapermen and editors were flattered with prepaid all-expense trips to Japan. The Japs neglected to mention to them that American news correspondents in Japan were subjected constantly to the most persistent spying of their every movement. Correspondent Newman sailed from Japan in November 1941, one step ahead of the Japanese police.

International Correspondence for Enlightenment on the Jewish Question.

Payments:
Germany:
Dresdner Bank, Depositenkasse H. Frankfurt a. M.
Postal cheque-account: Frankfurt a. M. No 6201
Hungary:
László Levatich, Postal saving's bank-account Nr. 40705, Budapest.

Publisher: Dipl.-Ing. A. Schirmer
Editor: Erich Schwarzburg.
Adress: "World-Service", Frankfurt a. M., Box 600.

New subscription prices
6 months – 1.25 Dollars (U.S.A.)
5.– sh. (Engl.)
12 months – 2.50 Dollars (U.S.A.)
10.– sh. (Engl.)

The reproduction of th[illegible] bulletin is permitted and desired, provid[illegible] that the source of information is [illegible] "World-Service" and the Publishers receive [illegible] copies of any newspaper containing items reproduced

— Bulletin published twice monthly in 11 languages. —

No. VII/18. 15. 9. 1940

**A halfmonthly bulletin issued in 11 languages:**

German edition:
**Welt-Dienst**
English edition:
**World-Service**
French edition:
**Service Mondial**
Russian edition:
**Міровая Служба**
Hungarian edition:
**Világ-Szolgálat**
Spanish edition:
**Servicio Mundial**
Dutch edition:
**Wereld-Dienst**
Rumanian edition:
**Serviciul Mondial**
Danish edition:
**Verdens-Service**
Norwegian edition:
**Verdens-Tjenesten**
Swedish edition:
**Världs-Service**

## CONTENTS.

1. **Winston Churchill's Forefather, the Duke of Marlborough, and the Jews together robbed the English Nation.**
2. **A new Jewish Poison Factory in New York.**
3. **Even Mohammed was advised to protect himself from the Jews.**
4. **The Pan-Islam Movement, in its Fight for Freedom, has come to a Final Decision against the Jewish-English Oppression.**
5. **And now the Jews must save England.**
6. **Rumania defends herself against Jewry.**
7. **Thirty Thousand Hectare Jewish Land in Hungary appropriated.**

WELT DIENST was the principal fountainhead for all Nazi propaganda to the suckers abroad. It was printed in nineteen languages and was distributed throughout the world by the **Ausland** Deutches Institut, a Nazi organization devoted exclusively to spreading Nazism and Pan-Germanism abroad

The Japanese, through American dummies, purchased two respected American magazines to get over their propaganda in themes such as these:

1. America has no interest in participating in a war because she is not being threatened.
2. The Greater East Asia Co-Prosperity Sphere doesn't threaten American interests.
3. Japanese are fighting China because the Chinese are Communists.
4. The Japanese have no imperialistic aims anywhere.

As the Japanese walked into one Pacific location after another, their propaganda went along. The natives first were impressed into slavery and then were told by the Japanese radio how well off they were and how victorious the Japanese continued to be. This line was droned with deadly repetition even after the Japanese were suffering one military and naval reverse after another.

When we finally did get into the shooting part of the war. the Japanese propaganda didn't lose its line or its motion. It added a special broadcast to American forces in the Pacific. Like the Germans' Axis Sally, the Japs added a "bedroom voice" calling herself "Tokyo Rose," who sounded like a girl from Connecticut. Here is a typical line she handed out:

"Hello boys; this is Radio Tokyo about to broadcast the Zero Hour in honor of the forgotten American soldiers, sailors and marines out here in the

Pacific. Here's a tune you'll like: Harry James playing, 'I'll Be Seeing You'."

After the record—which, incidentally, was one of the latest and reached Tokyo via "neutral Argentina"—Tokyo Rose would give out with some "innocent chatter" which went like this:

"But that girl back home isn't waiting to see you. She's out drinking with some 4F who's rolling in easy money. Maybe they'll have supper too. Mm-m-m-m, wouldn't a nice thick steak taste good right now, in some air-conditioned café? But you won't get any of that for a long time out here, Anyhow, here's another song. . . ."

Innocent sounding? Not labeled propaganda? It was as deadly to the homesick American soldier as if he had been killed and buried on a Pacific Island.

Even in defeat the Japanese were handing us a long line before our troops finally occupied Japan. In one instance, their broadcasts to us reported the Japanese Prime Minister's speech to the Japanese people as saying, "You have been defeated and you must accept defeat and co-operate with the Allies." But our monitors of the Federal Communications Commission heard the Prime Minister's speech to the Japanese people as broadcast on the Japanese domestic radio, and the alert monitor didn't hear him mention either "defeat" or "co-operation with the Allies."

If the bulk of the Japanese people know now that they're defeated, their propaganda-trained minds understand that it is only temporary. They are mentally attuned to await their next opportunity—if we are fools enough to give it to them.

That Japanese General who surrendered Shanghai meant every word when he said:

"The Japanese people will be ready for the next war in twenty-five years!"

We accelerated the surrender of the Japanese with the atom bomb, but no scientist or group of scientists has yet invented any military weapon which can blast an idea from the minds of a propaganda-saturated people whether the idea is labeled "Made in Germany" and comes from a willing fraulein, or if it is stamped "Made in Japan" and comes from a cut-rate geisha girl.

# IX
# AMERICAN PSYCHOLOGICAL WARFARE IS BORN

As the last few hundred men of the battered, tired and beaten remnants of the British Expeditionary Force waded or swam to the rescue boats in June 1940, Royal Air Force planes flew over them on the Dunkirk beaches to take a parting shot at the victorious Germans.

Only a few of the planes carried explosives. Most carried the seeds of ideas destined to grow into a full-blown resistance movement, which would harass the Germans for the next four years. These seeds were in the form of leaflets, printed in both French and German. It informed the people of France that their Allies would return and remove the Nazi yoke. It warned the Germans of the same promise. But more important, the leaflets implanted the idea of a nationwide resistance movement.

From the studios of the British Broadcasting Company, General Charles De Gaulle followed up the leaflets with a call to every Frenchman for resistance until sufficient strength could be gathered by Britain and other Allies.

At that moment, even though France's defeat was as great a tragedy to America as it was to France and all of the world, the United States of America stood with hands motionless at its side and its voice silent except in sympathy. America had no official propaganda organization, just as it had none in 1933, to strike back and neutralize the enemy poison.

Thanks to the foresight of President Roosevelt, the first step in that direction was taken with the formation of the official propaganda agency: The U. S. Co-Ordinator of Information. It was not until March 1942, that the United States Office of War Information and its overseas branch became a reality. Elmer Davis, the nationally-famous radio commentator, became OWI's first and only Director. Robert Sherwood, the playwright and speech-writer for President Roosevelt, became the director of the OWI's overseas branch.

Putting a warring nation's propaganda machinery in the hands of civilians was nothing new in the history of warfare. The British had done it successfully in World Wars I and II. The Germans, following Professor Banse's advice, did it in World War II.

OWI began organizing a broadcasting network for short wave transmission overseas and within a year had twenty-six radio transmitters sending out information to the world in twenty-five different languages and dialects. It was called "The Voice of America," and soon the world, including the enemy on both sides of the world, knew that "The Voice of America" was the voice of truth.

Our best weapon turned out to be plain, simple news—the very news which we freemen sometimes forget is not available to everyone. But we had yet to make our first battle contact in psychological warfare with the enemy. The moment of first face-to-face propaganda contact on a field of battle came a few hours before our troops landed in North Africa on November 7-8, 1942.

Before eighteen OWI civilian news and radio specialists landed with the Allied Expeditionary Force, we broadcast to the French civilians and soldiers from a radio station temporarily set up on the forward deck of the battleship *U. S. S. Texas*. We cut in on a French wave length and we told the French that we came as friends. We repeated President Roosevelt's own words in French which explained we came as liberators and not conquerors. The same speech was re-broadcast at least 100 times from OWI's "Voice of America," beamed from the transmitters on the east coast of the United States to all of Europe and North Africa.

After we had given the Colonial French this dose of psychological warfare, the military and naval commanders decided that although our word war had lessened resistance considerably, other means would be necessary to cover the landings and cut casualties. As a result these were the closing words of the battleship broadcast:

"You have been listening to 'The Voice of America' broadcasting from the forward deck of the American battleship *Texas*. The next voice you will hear will be the 16-inch guns of the *U. S. S. Texas!*"

Not long after the landings, the top military commanders took notice of the effective work of the American civilians in uniform. General George C. Marshall publicly commended them and General Dwight D.

Eisenhower announced the organization of the Psychological Warfare Branch, Allied Force Headquarters. It directed that the organization be strictly Allied, as were all military operations in the North African campaign.

The personnel of PWB-AFHQ consisted of American civilians (OWI), officers and enlisted men, and British civilians who came from the British Ministry of Information, the British Broadcasting Company and from the British Foreign Office. There were British officers and enlisted men in addition. At its peak, PWB consisted of 4,600 British and American workers.

Because Americans had had little or no experience in the field of propaganda, either in peacetime or wartime, many mistakes were made. For example, there was the wonderful program devised and launched among the North African Arabs, which went smoothly—so much so they became America's firmest friends. This program effectively scotched Nazi agents and radio broadcasts to the Arabs. But no sooner did the war move on than the program was dropped like yesterday's newspaper. The result: The friendship turned to mild enmity, which may or may not be overcome in the future.

But we learned our lessons quickly. Soon PWB became as professional as seasoned 20-year veterans. PWB used leaflets, radio, news, news photographs, special publications (produced in America and in North Africa); public address systems mounted on special trucks, which also showed American propaganda films; and documentation centers. These latter were really propaganda shops which OWI men shortened to call "prop shops."

In a short time OWI had built the United Nations Radio Algiers (with New York's WABC transmitter), and had taken over the powerful French Radio Tunis. Programs were sent into the heart of enemy-occupied Europe on medium and short wave in five different languages. There were frequent rebroadcasts of programs from "The Voice of America" and from BBC.

Combat teams, manned by OWI personnel, went into the field with the armies. They carried with them mobile printing equipment and radio receiving sets and they went about the business of throwing "paper bullets" at the enemy. But they received opposition from an unexpected quarter: from American combat field commanders!

The OWI-PWB men were thought by some generals to be psychiatrists who had come to the front to treat cases of battle neurosis among soldiers. In some instances the generals exploded with a speech like this:

"Look, you confetti soldiers! I've had this division for 20 months teaching them how to kill the enemy with rifles, machine guns, hand grenades and mortars. You'll ruin their morale if you show them how prisoners can be taken with little pieces of paper. Why don't you go and cut your paper dolls back in Algiers?"

But that opposition was overcome when the general officers saw live German and Italian prisoners, who could have stayed on to shoot at us, but instead stopped shooting and were taken prisoners with the "paper bullets." The generals also discovered that "live ones" talk and frequently give valuable information.

The American field commanders were completely sold on the "paper bullet" idea when they learned that the safe conduct passes or *Passierschein* which failed to reach the enemy, frequently were retrieved by fearless Arab boys who ignored both Allied and German mines. These boys then would sell them to German and Italian soldiers at black market prices.

The Caid of Bizerta verified this to Allied officers, adding that there never seemed to be enough safe conduct passes to meet the demand.

The passes were simply leaflets which called on the Germans or Italians to surrender, reiterated that their military position in North Africa was hopeless and instructed them how to use the pass. There was always a printed box in English which instructed any Allied soldier to feed these enemy soldiers, give them medical attention if they needed it and then send them to a safe place in the rear—enclosed, of course, with barbed wire.

These Allied safe conduct passes, which early in the war looked like just another handbill, wound up in the last stages of war looking like a college diploma engraved on bonded banknote paper. They were magical items. Fond Italian papas and mommas, instead of giving their conscripted sons a pair of warm socks as a parting gift, gave the new soldier an Allied safe conduct pass, purchased on the black market. It was presented to the boy with a firm parental warning to use the pass at his earliest opportunity.

More than one wise Italian parent found that such pass was the best life insurance they could buy for their war-bound sons.

The best testimonial to the effectiveness of the Allied leaflets came from the enemy. Colonel Orlando Figante, commanding the Italian 158th Regiment, told General Wavell after he was captured in Libya:

"Your leaflets worked to destroy our resistance, especially in Bardia. The troops spread them and were demoralized. They brought the leaflets to their officers for explanations. We could not give them any. The troops felt they had been tricked into the war."

The leaflets were fired at the enemy in the early stages of the war from British 25-pounders. Later, several types of artillery were used with a special shell case which protected the leaflets from burning or tearing before they reached the desired target. They were also dropped by the hundreds of thousands by planes. Of course, there was much initial opposition from the Air Corps. Pilots didn't see why they should risk their lives to drop pieces of paper rather than explosives.

But when a pilot saw the huge bag of prisoners taken as a result of a few thousand leaflets he had thrown, he too became an enthusiastic "spitball" or "nickel" thrower. After a while, the airmen referred to prisoners taken as a result of the leaflets they dropped as "my prisoners." That was fine with everybody because no one cared who claimed what as long as there were prisoners and they were behind barbed wire.

In January 1943, a group of Italians in Tunisia ran over to the American lines waving safe conduct leaflets which told "the story of our landings in North Africa."

"We didn't know you Americans were in North Africa," they said. "If we'd known that we would have surrendered long ago. We haven't got a chance."

Near Gabes, North Africa, an entire Italian tank battalion, but without tanks, surrendered to American forces without firing a shot. They admitted they had decided to surrender after seeing one of our leaflets.

Because the American leaflets were hurting the Germans where it hurt the most—in the minds of their superbly trained soldiers—they took drastic steps to curtail mental sabotage. The French defeat proved that the best-trained soldier, lacking the will to fight, is a perfect candidate for a military cemetery. A German deserter revealed that after seven men had deserted from the 69th Infantry Regiment an order was issued that if further desertions took place every tenth man would be shot.

A German court-martial sentenced one soldier to five years of hard labor for not delivering one of the Allied leaflets to his superior officer. The sentence was ordered posted on all unit bulletin boards. Knowing better than any military command the sledge-hammer effect of leaflets, the German High Command took strong measures to counteract Allied leaflets.

Troops were warned against "this poisonous flood" and were ordered to hand over all enemy leaflets at once to their officers. A handbook was issued to all German officers, titled, "The Officer as Leader in the Fight Against Enemy Propaganda."

When the Allied military leaders realized the powerful "fourth fighting arm" they had at their disposal, they took full advantage of "paper bullets." General Sir Harold Alexander, General Eisenhower's British

OFFICE OF WAR INFORMATION

UNITED STATES GOVERNMENT

SECRET

AMERICAN EMBASSY

LONDON

EFFECT OF ALLIED LEAFLETS ON THE MORALE OF AXIS TROOPS IN SICILY, PANTELLARIA AND IN NORTH AFRICA

The following sample of statements made by German and Italian Ps/W on the effect of Allied leaflets has been culled from various official reports. All the statements are indirect quotations except where direct quotes are used. The extent of the effect can be gathered from the PWB Report dated 1.7.43 to the Chief of Staff. Between May 20th and July 1st 20,207,000 leaflets have been produced by PWB, and 13,550,000 have been dropped by the Air Force.

Report from General Eisenhower's Headquarters, 26.3.43.

Italian P/W (private) stated that his unit found copies of the Allied leaflet 'Tripoli e Caduta'. They discussed it and decided to surrender if opportunity offered. When the Americans attacked on March 23rd, the unit surrendered without firing a shot. This story was confirmed independently by a sergeant of the same unit.

G-2 Reported 15.4.43. Headquarters 2nd Corps.

"Battle of El Guettar: Propaganda: Throughout the operations prisoners of war confirmed the effectiveness of propaganda leaflets. Such leaflets were supplied through the Psychological Warfare Branch of AFHQ, in any desired volume."

Cable 26.4.43 from AFHQ.

A German P/W captured by the 2nd Corps pulled an Allied leaflet from his pocket and said: "This is all true. This is why I surrendered."

An Italian P/W (Major) produced a leaflet as soon as he was captured and stated that they had a depressing effect on the enlisted men.

**The effect of Allied leaflets on the enemy was carefully reported to all units of the United States Office of War Information working in the psychological warfare field. This report kept the OWI London outpost informed on events in the Mediterranean theatre.**

deputy, personally requested a five-day leaflet barrage against the Germans and Italians retreating northward from Sfax.

A G-2 report from the headquarters of the Second Corps paid this tribute to psychological warfare during the Battle of El Guettar:

"Throughout the operation prisoners of war confirmed the effectiveness of propaganda leaflets. . . . It saves American lives. And that's the best it could do whether you call it tactical or strategic."

Before we took Sicily, it was necessary to capture the island of Pantellaria. The Italian commander first learned of the Allied forces' invitation to surrender from a leaflet dropped by one of the bombing planes. The second surrender letter was also dropped as a leaflet. Before he knew that Allied landing forces were approaching, on June 10, 1943, the enemy commander ordered the white flag and the white crosses put out the next morning, as the surrender letter directed.

Seven million leaflets were scattered on German and Italian positions as a preparation for the invasion of Sicily on July 10, 1943 (operation: Husky). Headed "Capitulation with Honor," the leaflet was written by top rank Allied generals and OWI men assigned to the PWB combat teams. The millions of leaflets flooded the enemy lines within seventy-two hours after they were dropped by Allied strategic and Tactical Air Forces.

Word warfare met with almost instant success in Sicily. The intensity of "paper bullets" was the greatest achieved by any army in either World Wars I or II up to that moment. In one sector where forty rounds of leaflet shells were fired in quick succession, seven

German soldiers came over to the Allied lines within a few minutes waving the leaflets in token of surrender.

A total of sixty-five of the first 100 prisoners taken at this point of the line had Allied leaflets on their person, the majority having hidden them in their boots to avoid severe punishment by their officers.

No single leaflet or series of leaflets will win a war or battle without the accompanying sacrifice expended by the infantry, the artillery and the air force. But these leaflets gave the fighting soldier a big boost in his uphill battle.

Here is a typical example how one little word after another given to the right people at the right time makes a tremendously effective "paper-bullet." It was distributed to the enemy within a few hours after slugging Allied forces had bottled up what was left of Rommel's Afrika Korps and the Italian African division into Cape Bon, Tunisia:

"TRAPPED!"

> "The German troops were trapped at Stalingrad. They were fighting very bravely. More, than 200,000 of them are dead. About 100,000 of them, amongst which there were Field Marshal Paulus and 21 generals, have surrendered.
>
> "For whose good did so many find heroic death?
>
> "It did not help Germany, now fighting against the whole world in arms . . .
>
> "Did it help the wives and mothers?
>
> "Did it help the soldiers themselves? According to Hitler it was their duty to

die. But the German people say to all young Germans: 'Live for our future.'

"TRAPPED!

"You are trapped in Tunisia too. The more German soldiers are enticed into this trap, the more satisfied we shall be, as one of these days the trap will be closed.

"WHAT WILL BECOME OF YOU?

"Do you want to go home? Do you want to see your loved ones again?

"Prisoners remain alive and see their homes again . . . so for you there is one solution—

"SURRENDER!

"This leaflet enables you to go through our lines. You will be well treated and received. At the end of the war you will go back to Germany. Use this leaflet. You will not be the first to do so by any means. There is only one solution—

"PASS (PASSIERSCHEIN)

"TO BRITISH AND AMERICAN OUTPOSTS: Any German soldier presenting this safe conduct is to be disarmed and made prisoner."

This type of leaflet was infectious. Another leaflet of this pattern, but addressed to Italian soldiers, caused the spread of the surrender contagion to Major Antonio Vassalini, who quit in March 1943, in Tunisia, with the help of an Allied safe conduct leaflet.

His explanation of how he came upon the safe conduct leaflet is amusing. An Arab had picked it up and had given it to one of the major's sergeants. A dutiful soldier, the sergeant obeyed a standing order to turn in all enemy propaganda to his commanding officer. Major Vassalini read it, believed it, and surrendered.

Six days after we landed in Sicily, we injected a necessary political element in the military phase of our psychological warfare. We set out deliberately to knock Mussolini from his tottering perch and, if possible, knock Italy out of the war. We succeeded in doing both—with the aid of psychological warfare, which included the leaflets and radio.

On July 16, 1943, millions of leaflets bearing the joint message of President Roosevelt and Prime Minister Churchill to the Italian people were dropped in every part of Italy. The Italian people were asked to make a choice between dying for Mussolini and Hitler and living for Italy. Mussolini hurriedly met with Hitler on July 19th. The same day Rome was bombed by Allied planes just as leaflets had promised. On July 25th, Mussolini was forced to resign.

The unconditional surrender of Italy was announced on September 8, the day before American troops landed on the Italian mainland at Salerno.

As in the Sicilian invasion, OWI leaflet men in PWB teams landed on the Salerno beach (operation: Avalanche) with the second wave of American troops of the Fifth Army under General Mark W. Clark. Within two hours of their landings, the confetti soldiers were producing "paper bullets" under enemy fire. The leaflets were addressed to specific units opposing our forces on the beachhead.

But the propaganda was not all in one direction. The enemy was busy, too, particularly on the Anzio beachhead, a place most Americans who served there would like to forget.

The Germans knew the British and American troops on Anzio were being mercilessly harassed. The beachhead was less than ten miles deep; its entire perimeter never exceeded twelve miles. From the heights of Castelgondolfo, the Germans had zeroed in the entire beachhead. A soldier was actually safer in a foxhole than in the hospital on the beach proper. There was no such-thing as "a rear echelon soldier." Everything was frontline.

German intelligence was alert and American soldiers were not always the souls of discretion after being taken prisoner. The Germans soon learned that the American soldiers were in a most unhappy frame of mind, and were, therefore, wide open to suggestion. The suggestions were not long in coming. The entire beachhead was sprinkled with German leaflets. They told the American soldiers that they didn't have to stay on the beachhead, and that a "fake" illness was as good a method as any in order to get out of combat.

The leaflets gave specific instructions on how to feign illness. The symptoms of at least a dozen ailments were carefully set forth, in easily understandable GI language. Soldiers were advised to seek out women and to contract venereal diseases. The "Naples-type" of gonorrhea was particularly recommended, because it did not respond to standard treatment.

These leaflets also told how easy it was to contract malaria in the beachhead area. The use of the prescribed U. S. Army "safeguards" was displayed as being "a nuisance." The leaflets also tried to persuade the men from taking their regular doses of atabrine and from using the mosquito netting.

But the Germans failed utterly in their attempt to induce American or British soldiers either to feign illness or to try to contract disease. And as one GI said to the author: "The kraut-sick leaflets couldn't have worked anyway. Our medics can spot a faker a mile away."

# X
# WORDS KILL AND CAPTURE

Thousands of American fighting men are alive today, thanks to little pieces of paper and words and ideas penetrating into the heart of enemy territory by radio, which is no respecter of blockades or Westwalls.

The little pieces of paper were from the huge newsprint tonnage which American and British newspaper readers were not getting in their "Daily Bugle," because newsprint also was at war. Many newspaper publishers griped worse than did the GI in a combat infantry outfit. The advertising they didn't get because the newsprint was lacking was busy advertising the virtues of surrender to German and Italian soldiers. If it's solace the publishers need, here it is:

More than 14 million leaflets were produced and delivered to German and Italian soldiers in the last ten days of the North African campaign. There were 33 separate issues in Italian and 32 in German. These leaflets helped precipitate the surrender of the enemy forces a full 28 days sooner than Allied intelligence estimated they could hold out. The result: more than 5,000 American and British lives saved because of a mess of newsprint.

For weeks before the invasion of Southern France (operation: Anvil) on August 15, 1944, Allied Air Forces literally swept the beaches clean of most enemy opposition with leaflets and special newspapers, notably the *Landser Post,* addressed to German troops guarding the coastal defenses. The material was written in German, Russian, Polish, Czech and in a few other Slavic languages because the French underground, which maintained the closest contact with Allied Force Headquarters, reported that the Germans had manned the defenses with impressed troops of all nationalities.

When the first waves of troops hit the Riviera more than 2,000 of these impressed troops, wearing German uniforms, surrendered to our forces. The payoff was calculated this way: how many American and French soldiers did *not* die because 2,000 fewer of the enemy were behind coastal guns, or rifles, or machine guns?

Summing up the phenomenal success of "paper bullets" in the southern France landings, the propaganda chief of Anvil, a 45-year old Manhattan newspaperman assigned by OWI to PWB, reported:

"We went from D-day to D-plus-70 in three days!"

By this time the use of psychological warfare had become an integral part of all military operations, although here and there a skeptical staff officer could be found. A corps commander on the British Eighth Army front in Italy was definitely one of those skeptics until he tried a little experiment of his own.

The Corps commander visited a prisoner-of-war cage and walked among the German prisoners with an interpreter at his side. A German prisoner was picked at random.

"Ask the prisoner if he ever has seen one of our leaflets," the corps commander told the interpreter.

To the question, asked in German, the prisoner responded promptly, pulling out a copy of *Frontpost* as he began to speak:

"Yes, here is what caused me to make up my mind to surrender. There is an article which shows why Germany cannot possibly win the war, and at the bottom there is a query: *Why die at five minutes to twelve?* I asked myself 'Why?' and took the first opportunity to surrender. If I had seen this article two months ago, I would have surrendered that much sooner."

After that, the corps commander ordered leaflet deliveries on his sector of the front stepped up ten-fold.

Leaflets sometimes do peculiar things, as in the instance of the Allied bombing of Rome. A real panic was produced when Allied leaflets announced that the city was to be bombed. When the explosives did fall pandemonium reigned. The leaflets gave the reasons for the bombings and as a result the blame for the bombing was not put on the Allies, who dropped the explosive, but on Mussolini and the corrupt Fascist government which had betrayed Italy to the Germans.

One German lieutenant captured in Italy talked about leaflets soon after his capture. His readiness to talk was remarkable, because few if any German officers volunteered information. Usually they denied everything on general principles.

He said: "Here is what happened in my unit one day not long ago. A non-commissioned officer handed me an Allied leaflet with the comment: 'These are just a lot of dirty lies!' However, I realized that he was not entirely convinced, so I pursued the subject further. Finally he broke down and said: 'I know, Herr Leutnant, that all of this is just propaganda, but they mention names and actual happenings in our own regiment. How can they know these things? They must have tremendous power. I feel as though they were everywhere.' Yes, in spite of all we can do, your leaflets are read by our men and have a damaging effect on their morale."

*Frontpost,* which was actually a newspaper rather than a leaflet, had exactly that effect on German morale because it was so widely read and believed. It was so valuable that in barter it was worth five cigarettes. Some idea of the value placed on this little newspaper can be had by recalling that the German soldier was issued only three cigarettes a day.

*Frontpost* was the little German-language newspaper distributed bi-weekly on the Italian front by shell and by air with a total circulation of several million copies weekly. It lived for fourteen months and its reputation for truthfulness and reliability was its greatest asset. Prisoners told Allied interrogators that in the early days *Frontpost* was disbelieved and dismissed as "just another bit of propaganda." But as months went by, the Germans discovered that everything appearing in its columns turned out to be true. Frequently they checked *Frontpost* items with their own news releases. Its arrival was looked for eagerly by all German soldiers, some of whom, when captured, made suggestions which would have warmed the heart of even a thick-skinned American newspaper circulation manager. They suggested a more efficient delivery, naming places and times where it would be picked up more readily by German soldiers without being seen by their officers.

They even pointed out that if deliveries could be made before dawn, German soldiers could pick them up undetected by their officers.

Like any faithful newspaper readers, they often complained of the delivery service. One prisoner refused to march to a POW cage until he received a *Frontpost* issue of September 18th, which he insisted he had not received although the September 22nd issue was right on time. Another groused that there had been no delivery of *Frontpost* for ten days. He was told that bad weather had grounded "the newsboys"—the tactical air force pilots, who hadn't been able to penetrate the soup which frequently envelops Italian mountains at that time of the year.

Here are additional items which show how the news as a weapon of warfare can have an acid-eating effect on the minds of enemy soldiers:

German prisoners reported that Allied newspapers gave them the first news of the attempt on Hitler's life in July 1945. It was instantly believed because of the credibility established by previous issues of the Allied newspapers.

The "Moscow Conference" leaflet telling of Allied post-war intentions regarding Austria produced sensational effects in Austria and among Austrians in the German army.

In Northern France a poll taken among several thousand German prisoners during August and September 1944, disclosed that 25 percent were deserters and 90 percent of these had leaflets in their possession.

# DEUTSCHER SOLDAT!

Wir versprechen Dir kein Paradies, wenn Du gefangen wirst. Du kannst aber bestimmt auf das Folgende rechnen :

1. **ANSTÄNDIGE BEHANDLUNG,** wie sie einem tapferen Feind zusteht. Kriegsgefangene behalten Rang und Ehrenzeichen. Deine unmittelbaren Vorgesetzten sind Kameraden der Wehrmacht.
2. **GUTES ESSEN.** Als Kriegsgefangener bekommst Du dasselbe Essen wie unsere eignen Truppen.
3. **ERSTKLASSIGE KRANKENPFLEGE** für die Kranken und Verwundeten. Nach den Bestimmungen der Genfer Konvention erhalten Kriegsgefangene dieselbe Krankenpflege wie unsere eignen Truppen.
4. **POSTVERBINDUNG MIT DER HEIMAT.** Du kannst monatlich drei Briefe und vier Postkarten schreiben. Postverbindungen sind zuverlässig und verhältnismässig schnell. Du darfst auch selber Briefe und Pakete geschickt bekommen.
5. **BESOLDUNG.** Nach den Bestimmungen der Genfer Konvention haben auch Kriegsgefangene noch Anspruch auf ihre Besoldung. Für jede freiwillige Arbeitsleistung wirst Du extra bezahlt. Du hast auch das Recht, in den Lagerkantinen einzukaufen.
6. **BERUFSFORTBILDUNG.** Wenn Du es wünschst, wird Dir Gelegenheit zur Berufsfortbildung gegeben. Deutschland braucht nach dem Kriege gelernte Arbeiter.

**Ihr werdet als Soldaten behandelt werden. Nach dem Kriege kommt Ihr selbstverständlich nach Hause**

German soldiers holding out in Cherbourg had this leaflet dropped on their positions. The leaflet offers prisoners-of-war fair treatment, good food, hospital care, mail facilities, Geneva-convention prisoner-of-war pay and educational facilities. It promises also that they will go home after the war.

Most of them admitted that the leaflet made them desert. Of *all* prisoners, 35 to 40 percent carried leaflets at the time of their capture.

Psychological warfare words put on the air in the proper channel worked its limited magic, even at sea. The amphibious problem involved the entire Italian fleet immediately after Italy's unconditional surrender. For this feat, Maurice Pierce, Cleveland radio engineer on duty with OWI in North Africa, was officially commended.

Allied naval officers knew that Italian naval personnel were prohibited from listening to the Allied radio. This posed the sticker of how to get necessary instructions to the Italian fleet so that their ships would steam to designated Allied ports and out of the grasp of the Germans. Pierce solved the problem by working all night to change the frequency of the Allied psychological warfare transmitter in Algiers to the international distress frequency to which all ships must be tuned at all times while at sea.

The scheme worked. Within twenty-four hours all Italian warships cruised into the designated Mediterranean Allied ports. This prompted the Mediterranean edition of the U. S. Army's *Stars and Stripes* to comment:

"Words are cheaper than blood, and both are helping to win the war."

But sometimes psychological warfare is not the black magic which is attributed to it by army commanders, who insist that psychological warfare can do anything—or at least, most anything.

The situation arose as a result of psychological warfare's sensational success in talking 2,000 German soldiers into surrender at Cherbourg. The "hog-calling" or sound truck device was employed here. Appeals and threats were intermingled with persistent American artillery fire. Leaflets were fired at the Germans too. finally, the beleagured German garrison gave up.

The wide newspaper publicity produced two unfavorable reactions against psychological warfare. The combat troops, who had given the Germans a terrible beating and had paid for it with more than ordinary casualties, developed an understandable dislike for the psychological warriors and their product. The last people who wanted credit for assisting in the completion of the Cherbourg operation were the OWI men who participated in it. They, better than even the American soldiers themselves, knew that all the "hog-calling" had done was to accelerate the inevitable.

Yet some military leaders decided that psychological warfare was the magic formula for winning battles. They ordered the "hog-callers" for all kinds of situations, even when conditions were far from favorable for surrender appeals. When the "hog-calling" failed to produce results in spots where the technique was not warranted, they turned a sour face on all psychological warfare.

And these were practical military leaders, who wouldn't have dreamed of using a machine gun to knock out a German Tiger tank or a tommy gun to do the work of a 240-mm howitzer.

However, in Aachen the "hog-calling" technique again worked, but only because it was put into play after the Germans had been soundly beaten by the men who do the fighting and dying. Under the threat of overwhelming force poised outside this first large German city to be attacked by American troops, "the supermen" proved themselves to be lice with the hearts of mice.

Unique conditions sometimes play right into the hands of psychological warfare teams. In Brittany, a mobile radio broadcasting transmitter was set up by men of the Psychological Warfare Division, SHAEF, to "pied piper" Germans out of a fortified position by calling to them one by one to come and get their mail from a bag captured by our troops. The Germans surrendered singly as their names were called although from their almost impregnable position they could have slaughtered American troops had a frontal assault been attempted.

On the Fifth Army front the writer witnessed German surrenders produced by "hog-calling" in languages other than German. One such incident took place in Italy's rugged Serchio Valley. An American officer speaking in Polish advised a group of Poles, impressed into the German Army, to kill the German NCO, who was their squad leader, and to surrender. The line that convinced them went like this: "Recall what the Germans did to your homeland in September 1939, when they burned, ravaged and looted it without warning!"

It is quite certain that Ludendorff, the German Field Marshal of World War I, had World War II in mind when he wrote in a document, captured after the 1918 Armistice:

"There are times and situations when one ton of propaganda leaflets—skillfully prepared and properly placed—can do more damage than one hundred tons of high explosive."

It is just as certain that in his burning, blinding desire for Germany's world conquest in 1920, 1950 or 2000, he did not anticipate that the "damage" would be done to German troops.

The greatest tribute ever paid to Allied psychological warfare (and indirectly to America's amateur propagandists) came from the fount of all German propaganda masterminding, Radio Berlin, which said in a broadcast April 14, 1945:

"Allied propaganda influenced the military decision by sapping Germany's strength and . . . forcing the High Command to change its strategic plans."

All was not "lily white" in American psychological warfare. "Black operations" or "black propaganda" paid handsome dividends when the Americans became sufficiently expert to handle these tricky operations without backfire. British "black operations" had considerable success. The British "black" specialty consisted in operating radio stations purporting to come from inside Germany.

"Black operations" were primarily designed to win enemy confidence for a carefully planned future "kill." The usual method was to indicate that the broadcast was coming from a German, although not necessarily an official Nazi, source. The Germans tried it from time to time, in an attempt to force the resistance movements (in German-occupied territory) to betray themselves.

"Black operations" were not confined exclusively to radio broadcasts, although radio attempts were usually the most successful. The Germans attempted to turn the success of an OWI published newspaper to its own ends, but failed. An expertly written and printed, four-color newspaper, the OWI publication was well-known for its excellent war maps. When dropped from American planes, the newspaper, folded, was no larger than a dollar bill.

One morning, French peasants found the familiar-looking newspapers lying in their fields. The paper gave faint praise to the Allied cause and seemingly showed great fear of the German war machine. The peasants saw through the hoax almost instantly. The quality of the printing, particularly of the maps, was so poor that the peasants knew the newspapers could not possibly be from an Allied source.

The most successful Allied "black operation" was "Operation Annie," a black radio operated by a psychological warfare team of the American 12th Army Group, which ran "Annie" from Luxembourg as *Nachsender* 1212.

"Annie" operated for only the five final months of the war. She was on the air each night for four-and-a-half hours, with strikingly authentic war reports as if seen through German eyes, with remarkably accurate pictures of life at the front and at home from the German side of the line. There were also German folk-songs and Viennese waltzes.

There was nothing Nazi about the content of "Annie's" programs, but it was friendly to the Germans. Every German reverse was honestly reported. Before long, German commanders were listening to "Annie," to find out how their side was doing. It was the perfect bait because "Annie" was playing for bigger stakes than simply being newsy and folksy for war-weary German soldiers.

**IM WESTEN:**

**Der Westwall durchbrochen!**

**Über 1 000 000 Gefangene**

**seit der Invasion!**

**Anglo-Amerikanische Luftoffensive**

**vom Rhein bis zur Ostfront!**

**IM OSTEN:**

**Ostpreussen, Wartheland und**

**Schlesien überrannt!**

**Die „Ruhr des Ostens“ verloren!**

**Rote Armee tief in**

**Brandenburg, Sachsen und Pommern!**

Here is one case where a ton of propaganda leaflets can do more damage than one hundred tons of high explosive. With the kind of news reported on this leaflet, psychological warfare can't help but work.

**IN THE WEST:**

**The Westwall smashed!**
**Over 1,000,000 prisoners**
**since the invasion!**
**Anglo-American air offensive**
**from the Rhine to the East Front!**

**IN THE EAST:**

**East Prussia, the Wartheland,**
**and Silesia overrun!**
**The "Ruhr of the East" lost!**
**The Red Army deep in**
**Brandenburg, Saxony and**
**Pommerania!**

As "Annie's" authenticity became more solidly established, her boldness increased. She appealed for aid for luckless party leaders who found themselves surrounded. Hundreds of Germans and their equipment walked into these Annie-baited traps.

To German civilians, "Annie" offered tidbits by telling them the Allies were dropping false ration coupons. This would send German housewives off to raid store shelves.

"Annie's" payoff came soon after the Remagen Bridge was captured by Allied troops. "Annie" hinted that there was but one way open for retreat between the Bridge and Andernach, where American troops had taken a sizable beachhead. Although there was ample room to retreat over other routes, the German troops trusted "Annie" so completely that they followed her advice and thousands of them walked right into an American trap, and were taken prisoners.

The death of "Annie" was as realistic and as dramatic as her life. For several days previous, her staff kept reporting the approach of the Americans. One night there were shots in the studio while "Annie" was on the air. Then the sounds of a scuffle were plainly audible. The despised Allies were seizing "Annie's" transmitter!

Sergeant Hans H. Burger, a member of the "Annie" team reported that the last broadcast was a recording:

"There lies a crown
 Deep down at the bottom of the Rhine."

# XI
# JAPS SURRENDERED TOO

One sweltering day on Guadalcanal, where in August 1942, American forces made their first land battle contact with the Japs, an Army sergeant swung his tommy-gun quickly toward some moving bushes.

He saw a Jap crawl out. The sergeant was so surprised he didn't fire although the practice on Guadalcanal was shoot first and ask questions afterward. Questions were seldom asked because invariably the Japs were dead.

The scrawny, toothy Jap made no menacing move. Instead, he sidled over to the American sergeant, showed his buck teeth and a hissy grin. He handed the sergeant an American leaflet which was splotched with Japanese script, but contained a message in English reading:

> SECURITY PASS
> TO ALL MEMBERS OF THE
> UNITED STATES ARMED FORCES:
> The bearer of this pass is surrendering. He is to be treated courteously and escorted to the nearest commanding officer, who

will arrange for his transfer out of the combat area. He probably understands no English but he has been instructed to obey sign orders.

Commanding Officer of the
United States Forces

That little Jap was one of the first nine Japs to surrender in the Pacific war.

The surrender of the first nine began to convince skeptical army men that Japs do surrender, and what's more, the technique of psychological warfare against the Japs was no different from that used against the Italians and the Germans!

Bradford Smith, OWI's chief of Central Pacific Operation, in discussing American propaganda to Japan stated:

"The opinion has been expressed that the Japanese are impervious to propaganda. There is no evidence to support this view.

"Since 1868, when they abandoned feudalism and entered the world of nations, they have been persuaded by propaganda into a set of beliefs which they never held before. By exerting a thoroughgoing control over education, the rulers of modern Japan have persuaded the common people to worship their Emperor as a god, have turned mythology into history by treating as gospel the story of the Emperor's descent from the Sun Goddess, and have made people believe that Japan can never lose a war and that a Japanese will never surrender.

"Propositions so far from the truth could never be accepted by a people who are not susceptible to propaganda. There is therefore some hope that American propaganda can have an effect on the Japanese and can therefore help shorten the war."

Smith wrote that in the midst of our propaganda warfare against Japan, at a time when we were developing psychological warfare big guns. OWI built up its Honolulu outpost as the springboard for word warfare against the Japs. Because Honolulu's modern printing presses could do the job, millions of leaflets of the strategic type destined for Japan were produced there.

Radio Honolulu located on Oahu was juiced up to 100,000 watts to boom across the Pacific and join the radio barrage produced from sixteen OWI transmitters on the Pacific west coast. Nearly 1,300 programs a week in ten languages—Annamese, Burmese, Chinese, English, Filipino, French, Indonesian, Japanese, Korean and Thai—sparked across the Pacific. When OWI's 50,000-watt medium-wave giant was built on Saipan, it helped bounce these broadcasts right into Japan and her backyard.

Radio Saipan hurt the Japs painfully where it hurt most—in the ears and in the mind. A Japanese newspaper article acknowledged the failure of the Japs to jam American broadcasts from Saipan. The article complained that the Japanese people would have to "develop ears of iron and a death-defying faith against these voice bombs."

Even a desperate campaign by the Japanese domestic radio failed to thwart Saipan's signal. The campaign repeated over and over again to the Japanese:

"Please turn off your radio without fail as soon as this broadcast is over. Please do this to save

此の眞相を知れ

**Security Pass**

TO ALL MEMBERS OF THE
UNITED STATES ARMED FORCES:

*The bearer of this pass is surrendering. He is to be treated courteously and escorted to the nearest commanding officer, who will arrange for his transfer out of the combat area. He probably understands no English but has been instructed to obey sign orders.*

*Commanding Officer of the United States Forces*

(日本文裏面にあり)

We delivered this simple surrender pass to the Japs in the early days of the Pacific war. It proved that Japs do surrender. Soon, the Jap surrender trickle became a torrent as we drove deeper into the enemy's defense rim.

# TICKET TO ARMISTICE

USE THIS TICKET, SAVE YOUR LIFE
YOU WILL BE KINDLY TREATED

Follow These Instructions··

1. Come towards our lines waving a white flag.
2. Strap your gun over your left shoulder muzzle down and pointed behind you.
3. Show this ticket to the sentry.
4. Any number of you may surrender with this one ticket.

JAPANESE ARMY HEADQUARTERS

投 降 票

此ノ票ヲ持ツモノハ投降者ナリ
投降者ヲ殺害スルヲ嚴禁ス

大日本軍司令官

Sing your way to Peace pray for Peace

The Japanese "ticket" shown here, like most everything the Japanese offered, was phoney. Its ultimate use was as a souvenir by American marines and soldiers, who found the "ticket" excellent as barter.

some electric power and keep radio sets in service longer."

But the broadcasts continued and the estimated six to seven million Japanese radios capable of picking up Saipan, continued to pick it up. Our intelligence officers in occupied Japan have now verified this.

All psychological warfare in the Pacific was operated by OWI under the supervision and in cooperation with the four top military and naval commanders. As the combat teams of OWI civilians went into action or prepared for future operations, their boss, Elmer Davis, received a copy of a letter forwarded by Brigadier General Bonner Fellers, military secretary to General MacArthur. The letter had been written by Colonel Sydney Mashbir, the Army's foremost student of Japanese psychology. It read:

"I trust that no one will ever underestimate the part which the campaign of ridicule, so ably carried out by your PWB, played in bringing the Jap Navy out to be destroyed. You now have a brand new set of admirals all ready to commit suicide."

OWI men were particularly anxious to make their warfare succeed. They discovered that the best Jap was not, as most marines insisted, a dead Jap. The best Jap was a live one because live ones could talk and they talked their fool heads off. The reason? A Jap who surrendered considered himself—as far as the Army, the Emperor and his family were concerned—a dead Jap. He thought he could never again face his family or his ancestors after surrendering so he talked, since he was positive he couldn't be any worse off than he was.

Some of the hottest Jap military secrets in the Pacific came from Japs who had surrendered at the behest of either our leaflets or our "hog-calling" talks, the latter given by Americans of Japanese extraction, who did superb work in their country's behalf, and in some instances by captured Japs who wanted to see their less fortunate comrades live. One surrendered Japanese officer even led a mission of American fighter-bombers to point out vital Jap military spots for us to blast.

While we had little to talk about before our offensive got rolling in the Pacific except what we would do later with the ships, tanks, guns, planes and bombs which we were then making, later we could pick and choose our propaganda material when our successes rolled out one after another. These successes also turned the propaganda tide, for as Brad Smith explained:

"Nothing succeeds like success. Nothing makes propaganda as effective as military power. Now that we have a continuous string of victories in the Pacific to point to, propaganda can be useful to save lives, American lives: to obtain valuable military intelligence; to shorten the war."

By proving to the Jap that our successes were an actuality, (i.e., asking a starving Jap soldier on a bypassed island, "Where is the Japanese fleet?") and by showing him that living to rebuild Japan was better than dying for an Emperor, who apparently didn't care because the promised reinforcements and food never arrived, the Jap was whittled down to size and to surrender.

While early in the war we were taking Jap prisoners by ones and twos, the closing weeks of the conflict saw them coming over to our lines by the hundreds and thousands.

落下傘ニュース

昭和二十年六月二十三日（土曜日）

比島作戰最後段階に入る

米軍カ谿谷を快進

日本軍の投降者急增

ブルネイ地區占領

米軍既に建設作業に着手

日本軍の抵抗極めて微弱

三巨頭會談

伯林近傍で開催の豫定

白堊館發表

國民に責任を轉嫁

米"國土防衛策"を批評

激戰九日間

那覇飛行場を攻略

尼ケ崎を爆撃

各軍需工場猛火を發す

知米派の立場

ザカライアス氏放送

廣西省戰線活況

支那軍各地で猛進撃

「動かざるものは生きる權利なし」

日本軍の悲慘な山中生活

日本軍を急追

亞大陸沿海を完封

香港、西貢等を猛襲

米軍三百万

太平洋に轉進

新型戰鬪機

Rakkasan News No. 15

Copies of **Rakkasan** (Parachute News) were dropped throughout the Jap empire to Jap troops and civilians to weaken their morale by informing them of the true picture of the war. This Japanese, who said he ceased resistance because of **Rakkasan, is now enjoying a good meal.**

（第二頁） 第十五號 落下傘ニュース 昭和二十年六月二十三日（土曜日）

## ボルネオ上陸戰に米空軍完璧の協力

### 約束を果したケニー司令官

ケニー將軍

【マニラ廿二日發】米極東空軍の現司令官ケニー大將は一年半以上も前のこと、それは丁度マッカーサー將軍がブナ攻略戰に兵を進めんとしてゐたときであつたが、同將軍に對して

"余の空軍はほかのことは何もしなくとも、貴官の將兵をかならず小銃を背に上陸させて見せよう"

と固く誓つたが、當時ケニー將軍の部隊に從軍してゐた一新聞記者はそのときのことを回想しつゝ次の如く報じてゐる

聯合軍は先週日本軍が念入りに陣地を布き抵抗せんとしてゐたその真只中に敢然ブルネイ湾地區上陸作戰を敢行、しかもその損害は僅かに兵一名に過ぎなかつたがこのことはケニー將軍が今なほ曾ての約束を立派に果してゐることを最も有力に證明するものであらう

ケニー將軍は麾下の第十三航空隊を全部動員したばかりか更に第五航空軍をも一部これに加へて猛爆作戰を敢行し地上部隊の上陸に際しては日本軍がほとんど抵抗出來ぬまでに至らしめた

## 米ソ關係愈緊密

### ス首相米大統領に感謝

スターリン首相

【モスコー廿二日發】先週米ソ兩國は武器貸與協定成立第三週年紀念日を迎へたが、右記念日に際し、ソ聯のスターリン元帥はツルーマン米大統領に宛て感謝のメッセージを送り"今次の共同の闘爭を通じて米、ソ兩國間の友好關係は更に强化された"と次の如く述べてゐる

"歐洲戰爭期間中米國は武器貸與協定によりソ聯に對して武器、食料その他の物資を供給したが、この協定は對獨戰を勝利に導く上に重要な役目を果し、多大の貢献をなした……"

## "偉大なる指揮官"

### 英皇帝より授勲の栄

## 蘭印を解放せん

### 蘭、對日戰に十五万を派遣

マニラ放送

## 甦つたテニヤン島

## 素人劇團も誕生

### 商機は極めて活潑

不幸中の幸

テニヤン島

大人も勉強

## ドーリットル

### 再び太平洋戰線に

## 二世傷痍兵晴れの凱旋

### ホノルル市民の花輪に埋まる

## 印英間に電話線

フクチャン

# PSYCHOLOGICAL WARFARE BRANCH

## U.S. ARMY FORCES, PACIFIC AREA

## APO 500

| | |
|---|---|
| LEAFLET: | Newspaper "Rakkasan News", June 23, 1945 |
| LANGUAGE: | Japanese |
| DESIGNATION: | Rakkasan News No. 15 |
| TARGET: | Japanese Troops and Civilians Anywhere |
| REMARKS: | To Weaken Enemy Morale by Informing the Japanese of the True Picture of the War. |

---

PAGE 1

PHOTO: Prisoner who recently ceased resistance enjoys meal.

SUMMARY: Swift advance in Cagayan Valley, number of Japanese surrenders increases rapidly; Brunei area taken by MacArthur, Japanese opposition slight; Philippine planes continue blockade Asiatic coast, Hongkong, Saigon heavily bombed; Big Three Conference to take place near Berlin; Japan's military leaders shift war responsibility to civilians, American observer criticizes "home fortification" strategy (boxed theme-of-the-week); savage figthing for nine days on Okinawa, Naha airdrome captured; three million American troops on way to Pacific; B-29's bomb Amagasaki, fires started in war factories; additional orders placed for new type American fighter plane; Kwangsi battle front in China active, Chinese troops hold point on coast east of Okinawa; prisoner reports Japanese troops lead miserable lives in mountains of Philippines, states those who cannot work left to die; Captain Zacharias comments on removal of Admiral Ichire.

PAGE 2

PHOTO: Japanese craftsmen work at trade on Tinian.

CARTOON: Fuku-Chan

SUMMARY: Perfect coordination of U.S. Airforce at Borneo landing; General Kenney fulfills promise to General MacArthur; General Doolittle to Far Eastern front again; FEATURE: Tinian rehabilitated year after captured by Americans, business is now brisk;—(subheads) relief committee, adults go to school also, dramatic society formed, Tinian shopping center; Holland to send 150,000 men against Japan, Dutch submarines transferred to Pacific; triumphant return to Honolulu of wounded Nisei, citizens cover them with wreaths of flowers; Eisenhower receives medal from King George; telephone line between India and China opened.

This leaflet was a double-edge weapon: it gave seeds to the Kachins and also reminded them: "Wherever the Japanese go, they bring destruction. Wherever the Allies forces come, the field spring up green." Specific sowing instructions are given. The seeds are contained in the envelope made from the perforations on the right hand page.

Of course, the Jap didn't overlook his psychological warfare to our troops. But the Jap's "paper bullets" to our men were concentrated on pornography, featuring naked women with shapely breasts. On the back of such leaflets the Japs instructed our soldiers:

"Use this ticket, save your life, you will be kindly treated . . . . come towards our lines waving a white flag."

But the best the "TICKET TO ARMISTICE"—as the Japs titled it—could do was start a terrific demand for the "tickets" as souvenirs.

Even in his most desperate efforts, when the Japs attempted to drive a wedge between Australians and Americans by portraying an American soldier in bed with an Australian girl while the Aussie soldier was depicted in the right foreground sweating in a jungle battlefield, the Japs failed in their efforts.

Our news leaflets to the Japs actually worked, although they were disbelieved at first because the Jap soldier had been fed on a weak diet of rice and a strong diet of Jap victories which had never happened.

One of the most effective of these news leaflets was called *Ji Ji Shu Ho* (News of the Week), which name was later changed to *Rakkasan* (Parachute News). *Ji Ji* was produced in Australia and millions of copies were dropped on Japan weekly. Both *Ji Ji* and *Rakkasan* printed straight news with heavy emphasis on Japanese defeats.

But when our carrier planes blasted him in his island foxhole and our warships bombarded his pillboxes into rubble, the Jap soldier began to understand that someone had been kidding him.

Deep in the enemy-occupied Philippines, we were harassing the Jap with our messages of courage to the Filipinos, printed on books of matches, pencils, packages of needles and thread, which we dropped by plane or smuggled in by submarine. General MacArthur's message, "I shall return," was printed on all tangible gifts, prepared by OWI personnel.

Similar gifts were dropped during the Northern Burma campaign to the Shans, the Kachins and the Burmans, who took direct action as a result of these OWI gifts and leaflets. OWI also provided packets of seeds and salt, and while flying over the territory U. S. Army Pilots watched the crops from these seeds grow. The seed and salt packets, the matches, the needle and thread packs, displayed the U. S. Army Air Force insignia and the American flag in color. Hundreds of American airmen were rescued and led to safety by these new-found friends, who were influenced by the simple gifts.

The leaflets prompted the natives to hide their food and their bullock carts, thus hampering the Japanese retreat. In some cases the leaflets inspired the natives to ambush and kill Japanese troops.

Native leaders reported that these packets, plus the leaflet warnings, not only saved American lives but also the lives of the natives who stayed away from places we told them we would bomb in order to blast out Jap installations, The warnings also served to keep native labor away from the Japs when the enemy needed it most. Trackmen, switchmen and laborers between Myitkyins and Mogaung went off in droves "to visit relatives" or "took sick" when we warned the natives of our intention to bomb Jap railways communications.

American leaflets aimed at stiffening the resistance among the Chinese brought warnings from the frantic Japanese that Chinese failing to turn in the leaflets to Jap-controlled police stations in occupied China would receive the same punishment as spies. But the Chinese ignored their Jap "liberators." Our news leaflets to the Chinese created a black market demand which ranged as high as four to five thousand Chinese dollars per sheet.

We even printed surrender leaflets for the Japanese for use in giving up to Chinese troops. This brought the Japs to a point of screaming frustration and prompted them to give the lie to the legend they spread that "Japanese never surrender." They issued a directive to their troops explaining that "blindly believing enemy propaganda" was one reason for Japanese soldiers "intentionally falling" into the hands of the enemy.

Millions of leaflets were also dropped on the Chinese warning them away from cities and towns we planned to bomb. Thousands evacuated the marked cities—with a double effect. First, it saved the lives of the Chinese, and second, it deprived the Japanese of acutely needed local labor.

Since all psychological warfare is cumulative, our propaganda did not reach its peak of effectiveness until the beginning of 1945. The war of words against the Japs during 1944 resulted in more Japanese soldier surrenders than ever before, numbering in the tens of thousands. Many Japanese dead on the battlefield were found with our leaflets on their bodies.

The thousands of enemy civilians who surrendered on Saipan and Okinawa because of our warning leaflets, removed a worrisome complication from our plan of battle. When we warned the Okinawans to flee to the hills, they followed our instructions implicitly.

As the war progressed and the fury of our attack mounted, military commanders began calling for our leaflets in increasing quantities. They were used on Bougainville, Saipan, Noemfoor Island, Biak, Wotke, Tinian, the Philippines, Burma, China, Okinawa and on Japan proper.

The most spectacular and most extensive—and most successful—use of psychological warfare by either side during the entire war found the Japanese at the receiving end, and with drastic results for them. It happened during that critical and breathtaking period between the issuance of the Potsdam Ultimatum on July 26, 1945 and August 14, 1945, when the Japanese bowed in unconditional surrender.

American psychological warfare experts pulled out every stop on the propaganda organ to accelerate the end of the war and save thousands of American lives. America's crushing air, sea and land blows against Japan were exploited to the fullest through both radio and leaflets.

Probably the most spectacular single event was the advance announcement by the 21st Bomber Command of the 20th (Superfortress) Air Force, which told which Japanese cities had been marked for destruction by B-29 attacks.

This was psychological warfare even beyond the fertile psychological warfare thinking of the Germans in their early days of spectacular victories, including

[illegible]

[illegible]

[illegible]

[illegible]

**NDAI HKAI TUM ATSAWMSHA HKAI NHTAWM, YU LAJANG YANG GAW, GRAI AWNG KAJA NA RE.**

ကျွဲမျိုးစေ့ကိုကောင်းစွာစိုက်ပျိုးကြည့်ရှုရလောင်းပါက အသမတန်ထွက်ကူးနိုင်၏။

SHA MAI AI RAWT JOI 25 DARAM PRU NA MA AI

NSHUNG SHANG AI HTE RAU HKAI MU. DECEMBER SHATA GARAI N HTUM AI SHALOI HKAI RA AI. DAWNG MI DARAM GANG AI LAM NI HPE GALAW NNA HKAI MU. DAI LAM NI HTA 2 LATA PREN DARAM DIN NNA TUM LANGAI LANGAI BANG LET HKAI WA MU. HPUN TU PRUT WA AI HPANG HPUN LANGAI HTE LANGAI 4 PREN LAPRAN DE TU AI HPUN NI HPE BAW KABAI KAU RA AI. DE A PAWT NI HPE SHATA 2HPANG DE DAW SHA LU AI.

စားနိုင်သောဥ၂၁ဝိသာရရှိနိုင်သောမျိုးစေ့။

ဆောင်းဝင်စမှ ဒီဇင်ဘာလအကုန်ထိစိုက်နိုင်သည်။ ၁၃ပေ စီကွာသောအတန်းကလေးများပြုလုပ်၍ငှင်းအတန်းများ တွင်၂လက်မအကွာ၌မျိုးစေ့တစေ့ကျစီထည့်စိုက်ပါလေ၊ အပင်ကလေးများပေါက်သောအခါ တပင်နှင့်တပင်၃လက်မ ခန့်ထား၍ကြား၌ စိုပ်သောအပင်ကလေးများကိုနုတ်ပစ် လိုက်ရမည်။ ၂လခန့်အချိန်တွင် ဥများကိုနုတ်စားနိုင်သည်။

SI JOI 187 DARAM PRU NA MA AI.

SHAWNG NNAN NSHUNG AI KAW NNA DECEMBER SHATA GARRI N HTUM YANG HKAI TUM HPE BAN TAWN RA AI. BAN TAWN NGUT AI HPANG SHATA MI DIN DE DAI HKAI BAWNG NI HPE GADE NDE DAWNG 2 GANG NNA HTU KRAWK SAN TAWN DA AI NHKUN NI KAW HKAN HKAI MU. BAWNG NI HPE HTAWT HKAI AI KAW NNA SHATA MASUM DIN AI HPANG NSI HPE LU DI SHA NA MYIT DAI.

မှည့်သောခရမ်းချဉ်သီးအရေပိဿာအချိန်ကိုရရှိနိုင်သည့်မျိုးစေ့။

ဆောင်းတွင်းဒီဇင်ဘာလအကုန်ထိစိုက်နိုင်သည်။ ရှေးဦးစွာ မျိုးစေ့ကိုပျိုးထားရမည်။ တလအရွယ်ရှိသောပျိုးပင်က လေးများကိုတတွင်းနှင့်တတွင်း၃ပေစီကွာ၍ကောင်း မွန်စွာပြုလုပ်ထားသော ငှင်းတွင်းကလေးများတွင်ပြောင်း စိုက်ရမည်။ ပြောင်းစိုက်ပြီးသည့်နောက် ၃ လအချိန် တွင်အသီးများကိုချူးစားနိုင်သည်။

KHOL KOHL PAWT JOI 42 DARAM PRU NA MA AI.

NSHUNG JANUARY SHATA 15 YA DU HKRA GARA ATEN RAI TIMUNG HKAI TUM HPE BAN TAWN RA AI. LABAN BAT 3 DIN AI HPANG ATSAWMSHA LAJANG TAWN DA AI AGA DE DAI HPUN BAWNG NI HPE HTAWT HKAI MU. GADE NDE LADAWNG LADAWNG HKAI NNA HPUN LANGAI HTE LANGAI NI HPE HKAI RA AI. BAWNG NI HPE HTAWT HKAI AI KAW NNA SHATA 1 DIN DE DAI PAWT GINLANG NI HPE MAI SHA AI.

၄၂ ပိဿာအချိန်ရှိဥများကိုရနိုင်သောမျိုးစေ့။

ဆောင်းတွင်းဇန်နဝါရီလ ၁၅ရက်ထိမည်သည့်အချိန်မဆို စိုက်နိုင်သည်။ ရှေးဦးစွာမျိုးစေ့ကိုပျိုးထားရမည်။ ၃ပါတ် အရွယ်ရှိသောပျိုးပင်ကလေးများကိုကောင်းမွန်စွာပြု လုပ်ထားသောမြေကွက်တွင်တပင်နှင့်တပင် ၁၃ပေ အကွာတွင်ပြောင်းစိုက်ပါလေ။ ပြောင်းစိုက်ပြီးသည့်နောက် ၂လအချိန်တွင်နုနယ်သောဥများကိုနုတ်စားနိုင်သည်။

HPUN NHPANG 31 DARAM SHATUT LET, JOI 5 DARAM LI AI SHAPRE SI 1550 PRU NA MA AI. LANING MI 2 LANG MAI HKAI AI. NSHUNG TA NOVEMBER SHATA KAW NNA FEB. SHATA HTUM HKRA KALANG MI, SHING N RAI LANAM NNAN SHANG DE MAY SHING N RAI JUNE SHATA KALANG MI HKAI MAI NGGADE NDE DAWNG 2 PA AI LAMU GA ALAWK NI HPE LAWK LANGAI HTE LANGAI DAWNG 2 JAHKA NNA SHAWNG GALAW MU. LAWK SHAGU HTA DAWNG LANGAI MI JAHKA WA LET YUNG NU MI SUNG AI NHKUN 3 GALAW MU. NHKUN SHAGU HTA HKAI TUM 5 BANG NNA AGA HTE BAI KAPUT MU. HKAI HPUN PREN MI TSAW WA JANG NHKRUN JUN YU RA AI.. SHA MAI AI ASI HKAI.UNG NI HPE SHATA 3 NA JANG LU DI SHA AI.

ကျွဲမျိုးစေ့သည်အပင်ပေါင်း၃၁ပေါက်စေ၍ ၅ပိဿာအချိန်ရှိ သောပဲတောင့်ပေါင်းရေ ၁၅၅၀ ကိုရရှိနိုင်သည်။

တနှစ်လျှင်၂ကြိမ်စိုက်နိုင်၏။ ဆောင်းတွင်းနိုဝင်ဘာလမှဖေဖော်ဝါ ရီလကုန်ထိတကြိမ်။ မိုးတွင်းမေလမှဇွန်လထိတကြိမ်။ ရှေးဦးစွာ ၃ပေစီကွာ၍ အလျားအနံ၃ပေစီရှိသောမြေတွက်များကိုပြုလုပ်လေ။ ၎င်းမြေကွက်များအသီးသီးတွင်၁၃ပေစီကွာပြီး ...သောတွင်း ကလေးများပြုလုပ်ပါ။ တတွင်းလျှင်မျိုးစေ့၅စေ့ကျထည့်စိုက်၍မြေ မှုန့်များဖြင့်ဖုံးထားရမည်။ အပင်များလက်ခန့်မြင့်သောအခါ၎င်းတို့ အားပံ့ပိုးရန်ထောက်များဆောင်ပေးရမည်။ စိုက်ပြီးသည့် နောက် ၃လ အချိန်တွင်ပဲတောင့်နုများကိုချူးစားနိုင်သည်။

[illegible]

[illegible]

ANHTE DU AI SHARA MAGUP NDAI ZAWN HKAI
TUM KAMAN HKAN KARAN GA AI.
LU AI NSI NAISI GAW NANHTE A RAI NGA AI.
NANHTE SHA N MAT YANG ANHTE HPE DUT LU AI
NSI NAISI JOI 5 HPE GUMHPRAW DENGGA
LAP 5, SHING N RAI LABU LANGAI MI,
SHING N RAI JUM JOI 5 HTE GALAI
NGA GA AI.

NIPPON GINJANG NI DU
MADU KAW JAHTEN
SHABYAK MA AI.
ANHTE MUNG BAWNG
HPUNG NI DU AI
SHARA MAGUP SUN
HKAUNA YAWNG GAW
HKAI AMYU MYU HTE
TSIT LALI NGA AI.

နိပ္ပွန်တို့လက်ချက်ကျော့လေရာ
ပျက်စီးယိုယွင်းသည်ကိုတွေ့ရအံ့။
မဟာမိတ်တပ်သားတို့ရှေ့သို့
တိုးလေတိုင်းလယ်ယာချောင်း
မြောင်းတို့သည်ပြန်လည်စိမ်း
လန်းစိုပြေလတ်။

သွားလေရာ နေရာတိုင်းကျွန်ုပ်တို့အသမဲ့ ဟင်းသီးဟင်းရွက်
မျိုးစေ့ဝေလျက်ပင်။
ရရှိသောအသီးအနှံသည်အခင်းသွားအကျိုးသာဖြစ်၏။ ပိုလျှ
ံကြောင်းလိုက ကျွန်ုပ်တို့ဝယ်ရန်အသင့်ရှိ၏။
၁ ပိဿာအချိန် ဟင်းသီးဟင်းရွက်ကိုငွေဒင်္ဂါး ၁ ကျပ်။ သို့မ
ဟုတ်လုံချည်တထည်။ သို့မဟုတ်ဆား ၁ ပိဿာနှင့်ဝယ်မည်။

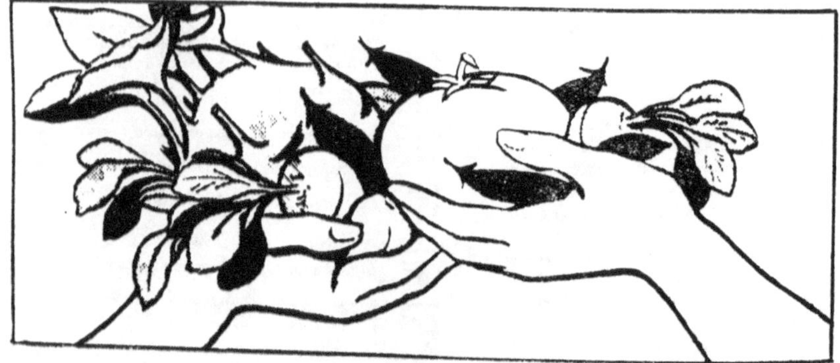

their defeat of France. This was psychological warfare hitting on all sixteen cylinders. OWI-prepared leaflets fell on eleven Japanese cities on July 27, warning the inhabitants that four of the eleven would be destroyed within the next few days.

The leaflets repeated to the Japanese people what we had told them many times before: "The United States is not waging war against the people of Japan but is battling the military machine which has enslaved the people of Japan."

The message warned the Japs to seek new leaders "and from this freedom will emerge a Japan that is new and better."

Four of the cities named were bombed as promised. Then, a second leaflet, prepared and produced by OWI and naming another list of cities was dropped on Japan, July 31st. A third bomb warning was scheduled, but it was never dropped. More momentous events made this third warning unnecessary.

On August 6, President Truman announced that the first atomic bomb had been dropped on Hiroshima. Transmitters in San Francisco, Hawaii and Saipan boomed the statement into Japan. For an unbroken period of three-and-a-half hours, the Japanese were told in their own language what had happened to Hiroshima and what they might expect in the future.

Strong emphasis was placed on the President's statement that "it was to spare the Japanese people from utter destruction that the ultimatum (Potsdam) was issued," and that if the Japanese "do not now accept the terms they may expect a rain of ruin from the air the like of which has never been seen on this earth."

This is the text of the first atomic bomb leaflets dropped on Japan:

"America asks that you take immediate heed of what we say in this leaflet. We are in possession of the most destructive explosive ever devised by man. A single one of our newly developed atomic bombs is actually the equivalent in explosive power to what two thousand of our giant B-29s can carry on a single mission. This awful fact is one for you to ponder and we solemnly assure you it is grimly accurate.

"We have just begun to use this weapon against four homeland. If you still have any doubt, make inquiries as to what happened to Hiroshima when just one atomic bomb fell on that city.

"Before using this bomb to destroy every resource of the military by which they are now prolonging this useless war, we ask that you now petition the emperor to end the war. Our President has outlined to you the thirteen consequences of an honorable surrender. We urge that you accept these consequences and begin the work of building a new, better and peace-loving Japan.

"You should take steps now to cease military resistance. Otherwise, we shall resolutely employ this bomb and all other superior weapons promptly and forcefully to end the war.

"Evacuate your cities now."

The radios came into play again repeating the message in Japanese over and over again. Even with the sharply restricted use of the radio receivers in Japan, the Japanese could not help but hear it, especially over OWI's Radio Saipan.

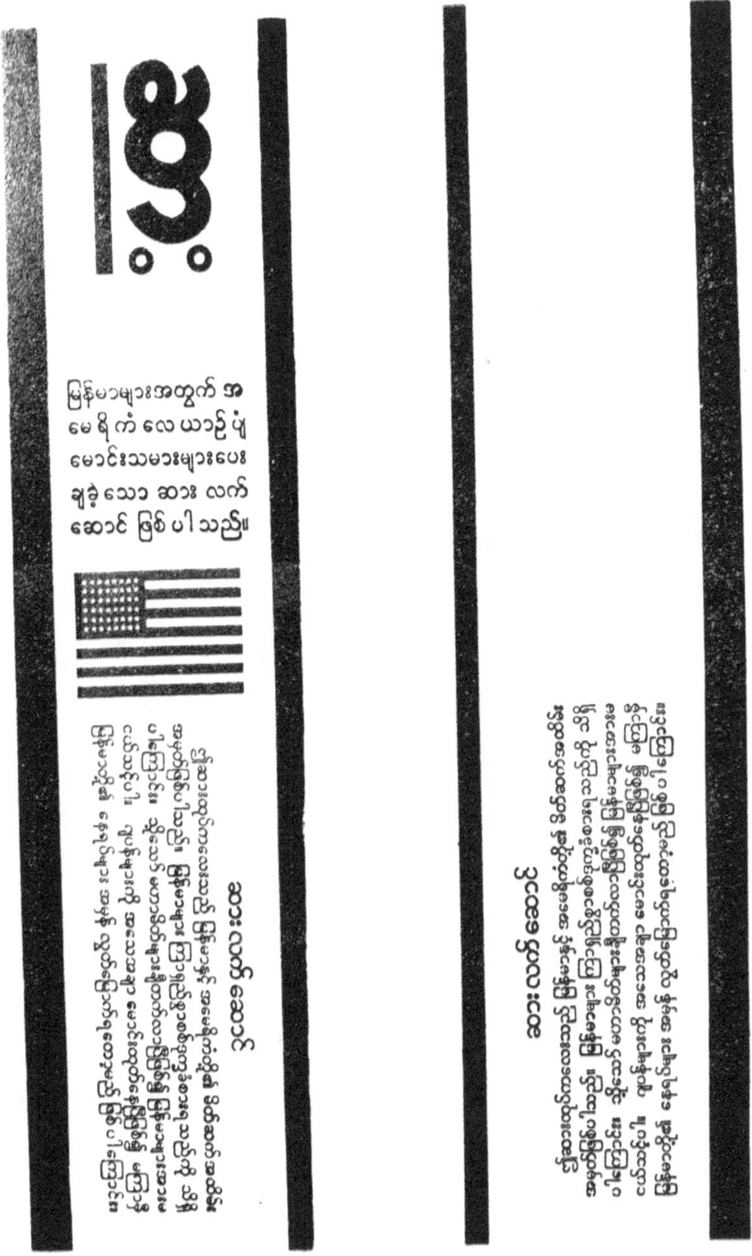


This red bordered message accompanied salt packets dropped to Burmese in eastern and lower Burma. It states: "This gift of salt comes from the crew of an American airplane. (U.S. Flag) This is a small token of American friendship for the people of Burma. We know your suffering has been long and hard. But take heart. The Allies are coming. The Japanese are being steadily driven out of Burma. The time will come when your place, too, is freed."

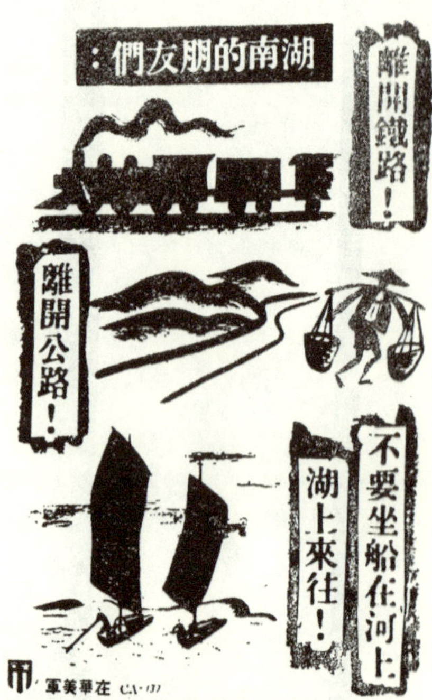


Written in Chinese and addressed to the people living, working or traveling along the Canton-Hankow railroad, this leaflet warned people against hauling or repairing for the Japanese to save their own lives from Allied bombings. This and others with a similar appeal slowed the Japanese advance—and retreat—considerably.

**保全你們自己的性命！**

今天，盟軍正把日寇自湘西趕走。在地上部隊推進之前，中美空軍會日夜不斷的轟炸和掃射粵漢鐵路，由寶慶到衡陽，長沙，岳州，漢口的公路，以至湘江，洞庭湖和長江。

盟機的目的在於殲滅日寇和把可以運輸日軍和他們的供應品的一切方法加以破壞。但是，自飛機放射下來的炸彈和槍彈，是不能把中國人和日寇分開的。

因此，請你們注意下列的好意的勸告：

不要在粵漢鐵路沿線工作。

不要在從寶慶到衡陽，長沙，岳州和漢口的公路上趕大車，做工或走路。

不要在湘江，洞庭湖或長江上坐船，或在那兒的碼頭上做活。

遠遠的離開鐵路，公路和水道吧！

The Okinawa battlefield was swept clear of all Japanese civilians by this leaflet, which sent thousands of them fleeing to the hills in accordance with instructions. Used also when American forces invaded other Jap-held islands, the leaflet headed, "Instructions to Island Inhabitant," stated: "Now that American forces are invading your island, your lives are in danger. Beaches will be bombed and shelled in order to weaken the Japanese Army and prepare for American troop landings. . . . Civilians who remain in coastal areas will be destroyed together with Japanese soldiers and installations used by the Japanese Army. If you value your lives, follow these instructions."

America's concentrated psychological warfare persisted with the announcement of Russia's entry into the Far Eastern war, for which leaflets had been prepared many days in advance.

When the Japanese Government seemed to hesitate in accepting the Potsdam terms, there was some feeling that perhaps a leaflet telling of the peace efforts would impede the surrender process by embarrassing the Japanese leaders in their obvious attempts to soften their own people for the blow.

However, the view that the full facts be given the Japanese people prevailed. A further reason for this decision was the feeling that the surrender messages would make the Japanese masses realize how hopeless were their chances of winning and thereby markedly lessen their willingness to continue the war should the Japanese Government change its mind and reject the Allied terms.

The leaflet was prepared by OWI men and representatives of the State Department, working through August 11th. In its final form the leaflet was telephoned to Honolulu for lettering and conversion into Japanese script. Within four hours, Honolulu had page-proof form for radiophoto transmission to OWI's printing plant on Saipan.

Voice broadcasts on both Honolulu and Saipan stations were interrupted to radiophoto the text. On Saipan the leaflets were printed, packed into leaflet bombs and loaded into B-29s, whose bombing missions had been cancelled to drop the special leaflet.

Approximately thirty-nine hours after work on the text had been begun in Washington, the leaflet was being dropped over Tokyo and the principal cities of

Japan. Within forty-eight hours, 5,500,000 of these leaflets had been dropped.

The leaflet's text was in three parts. An introduction, the Japanese surrender offer, and Secretary James Byrnes' reply on behalf of the Allies.

The introduction read:

"To the Japanese people: These American planes are not dropping bombs on you today. They are dropping leaflets instead because the Japanese Government has offered to surrender and every Japanese has the right to know the terms of that offer and the reply made to it by the United States Government on behalf of itself, the British, the Chinese, and the Russians. Your government now has a chance to end the war immediately. You will see how the war can be ended by reading the following official statements."

When President Truman's statement, announcing the Japanese capitulation, was issued at 7 p.m. EWT, August 14, 1945, it was nineteen days and a few hours after the issuance of the historic Potsdam ultimatum to the Japs. Thus, the weapon of psychological warfare, like the other weapons employed by the Allied forces, had completed its major assignment in World War II.

"How many do you have to indoctrinate tonight, Gretchen?"



This cartoon, reprinted by special permission of the New York newspaper PM, is an excellent description of how German females, still overwhelmingly in favor of Hitler and the Nazi way of life, will carry on their bedroom propaganda among American troops.

# XII
# WHAT TO EXPECT FROM GERMANY AND JAPAN

World War II is far from won.

The shooting is over, but we are a long way from achieving a total victory in a total war. We have won the military war on both sides of the world, but the psychological war remains to be won.

The Germans, no less than the Japanese, will not be changed overnight into peace-loving human beings, intent only on spreading the milk of human kindness throughout their countries and the world. Too little time has elapsed since the Japanese rape of Nanking and the attack on Pearl Harbor. What the Germans did to millions of innocents in murder crematoria, such as Belsen and Dachau, is all too recent.

Basically, the Germans and the Japs are on the same level now and will be for some years to come. That level is the lowest possible for any one supposedly classed as a human being to achieve. The military defeats of Germany and Japan are but unpleasant, inconvenient interludes for both nations. Deep down, under the cover of bowing, humility and groveling at the feet of the military conqueror, they are nursing the same hope they have nursed for scores of years: world conquest.

It should never be forgotten that it was the vote of the German people which made Hitler and his gang possible. The German people remain what they always have been: accessories before, during and after the crime.

The Japanese people were the ones who carried out the atrocities of China, the Philippines, Burma and in their own land. The fact that they now weep and insist they did it under orders and under the divine blessing of the Emperor, does not purge them or the Emperor of guilt for the crimes they perpetrated.

If we do not maintain vigilance throughout the world, including the United States of America, then the more than 201,000 American graves we have dug on the battlefields of the world will soon become a hollow mockery and a desecration of the memory of the men who fill those graves.

The Germans planned for defeat as carefully as they planned for victory. Of course, they didn't want to lose the war and were confident that they would win. But the Germans are careful, meticulous planners. They never make a move without calculating all eventualities. The slim possibility of their losing was carefully considered. That possibility came to pass and the plan for defeat was placed into operation.

Certainly, no German will tell us it is operating. After all, we are conquerors and occupiers and they must fawn over us as much as possible to obtain our immediate favors and then to lull us into an occupier's sleep. The plan was very simple when first formulated, but it was necessary to make certain changes to take care of changing conditions. Here is the original plan paraphrased:

"Guerrilla armies, numbering half a million fanatics, will continue armed resistance, particularly from the Alps; they will be supplied from well hidden, long prepared supply dumps. Thousands of specially trained Nazis will work illegally in Germany sabotaging the peace, destroying Germans who collaborate with the Allies, keeping aflame the fires of German nationalism and Nazi ideology.

"A small group of highly trained agents will operate *in other countries,* will propagandize for a square deal for Germans, then for the return of German property confiscated by the Allied governments, eventually for the resurrection of German cartels and industrial strength."

There is no doubt that thousands of Germans have gone "underground." While it is true many walk the streets—and without the SS uniforms—they have gone underground only so far as their thoughts are concerned. This makes them more dangerous, because just as they operated in the United States from 1933 through most of 1941 without a label, so are they operating in Germany today without a neon sign to identify them.

Their dirty work will begin with fawning over our occupation troops. They will be the most humble people in the world. Soon, their courage will get them to say they are "so sorry," that after all they "are good Germans." Some of this "good German" hooey has already begun to operate.

Hundreds of soldiers returning to the United States from Germany have remarked that the Germans are a clean, neat, well-dressed, well-fed people, and "so different from the dirty French, Italians, Czechs, Belgians, etc." But these American soldiers forget that the soap the Germans are using, the food they have eaten and the clothes on their backs, is the loot of Europe! And in many instances the loot from the bodies of the Belsen crematory victims!

And it is not easy to forget soap when we are reminded by incidents such as this one which took place early in December, 1945, in the Transylvanian town of Brashen. There the Jewish community performed the traditional Hebrew burial services over a case of soap, which was found in the town. The soap, which had been sent from the Reich to German settlers in Transylvania was inscribed, "Pure Jewish Soap." This soap had been made from fat obtained from corpses of Jews murdered in Nazi death camps.

Many soldiers and American civilians have already forgotten the mountains of shoes of all sizes, from baby size to the largest adult size, which our troops uncovered in German murder camp after murder camp.

The thing which amazes psychological warfare experts is the naïvete of Americans, military and civilian, whose memories are so short they forget that Germany declared war on the United States (Dec. 11, 1941), not the other way around. And that hundreds of American soldiers taken prisoner were treated not unlike the millions of innocent European civilians, deliberately starved and then slaughtered by the Germans between 1933 and 1945.

The entire German population, from the age of three up, have been trained in propaganda. The important part of Germany's plan in defeat is to use that as the strongest weapon against "the invaders and interlopers"—the occupation troops.

There has already begun a velvety subtle propaganda campaign to drive a wedge among all Allies in Germany. The Americans are cursed to the British, the British to the Russians, the Russians to both, and vice versa and criss-cross every way possible. Already the Americans are hearing:

"Germany's greatest salvation will be a war between America and the Soviets!"

This was exactly the pre-war and wartime propaganda line handed out by the Germans to get the Allies quarreling among themselves. It will be embellished with the explanation that the Germans had to fight this war to prevent Europe from going "communist." In America we were fed this pap by the Nazi-controlled German-American Bund.

Another "line" the Germans will use, will be, "Let's wipe the slate clean."

Such Nazi impertinence was launched within a few minutes after the Germans signed the documents of unconditional surrender. Colonel General Gustave Jodi, German Chief of Staff, told American, British and Russian signatories, when he was permitted to speak:

"In this war which had lasted more than five years both the German Army and the German people have achieved and *suffered more than any other people of the world*. Let us hope that the victor treats the German army and the German people with generosity."

Jodi was positively flabbergasted when arrested and indicted as a war criminal and stated for all the world to hear and gasp in amazement:

"Formerly when we lost a war we laid down our swords, traded a province and were friends. Now you seek to destroy us."

The Germans have always contended that when bigger and kinder fools are found, they'll be found in the United States of America. The German mind, including the military mind, cannot conceive that we are mad at them. After all, they say, "We good Germans didn't do it; it was the guy up the street. Where is he? Oh, he has disappeared. Probably blown up by Allied bombs." And so on and on ad nauseam.

Just to keep the record straight, here are some of the other "lines" the Germans are stringing to catch "the poor fish," and perhaps win psychological victory:

Europe cannot exist without industrial Germany. If you break up German industry, the peoples of Europe will suffer. *Bunk!* Because France, England, northern Italy and other spots throughout Europe, including industrial Russia, can supply Europe as well, if not better, than the Germans. And certainly not with the same intent as the Germans: keeping a huge civilian industrial machine going to make it quickly convertible into war production.

Germany wants peace and if she's given a chance to rebuild—with American money—she'll have no hostile intentions toward anyone. *Bunk!* Austria, Czechoslovakia, Norway, Denmark Luxembourg, France, Holland, their ruins and their dead stand as eloquent answer to that old Nazi chestnut.

Americans were in this war as suckers, fighting somebody else's war. *Bunk!* America fought this war defensively. She fought it in Europe so she wouldn't have to fight it in Pennsylvania, Florida or Massachusetts. We fooled Hitler's invading Army when they came to America in civilian clothes injecting poison into American minds; we picked up our six shooters in the nick of time. We have always been called "enemy" by the Germans.

The cruel and inhuman terms of the Treaty of Versailles forced us to rearm. *More Bunk!* The baloney about the Treaty of Versailles was one of Germany's biggest lies to the world. The terms imposed by Germany on Russia in 1917 by the Treaty of Brest Litovsk made the Versailles document look like a lost game of marbles.

The German isn't sorry for the 25 million dead he placed in their graves. And he certainly isn't sorry for the more than six million Jews and three million Poles he slaughtered.

Dr. Alfred Rosenberg, indicted war criminal and the Nazi Party's official philosopher: "The second German secret weapon is anti-Semitism, because if it is consistently pursued by Germany, it will become a universal problem which all nations will be forced to consider."

The poison of Hitler's lie about the Jews is still hanging over the world. Catholics, Free Masons, the organized Protestant Church in Germany and "International Bankers" were also used in Hitler's carefully planned program of scapegoatism, but with less publicity from the Germans.

The other big lie of the supremacy of Aryan blood, is one long since effectively scotched not only by the world's hematologists (blood specialists) but by the united front of every race, religion and color which helped to beat Germany.

The current German technique is to blame everyone higher up because, always, the Germans were committing their crimes on someone else's order. Eventually, by this phony reasoning, the blame would be placed squarely on Hitler's head. But Hitler is allegedly dead. So, reason the conniving Germans, no one should be punished. But the Germans forget, all too easily, that they voted Hitler and his gang into power!

Among occupation troops, German women will undoubtedly carry on the most deadly propaganda of all: bedroom propaganda. Yes, on these feminine heads falls a good part of the blame for yielding to the worst features of Nazism, including every aspect of racial cruelty, and also the Nazi orders that they produce as many babies as is humanly possible.

The most fanatic Nazis were, and are, women. Sigrid Schultz, American news correspondent in Germany for twenty-five years, places a good part of the blame for Nazism on the German women. Pan-German fanaticism comes to them naturally. At their grandmothers' knees, these women learned of the red-bearded Emperor Barbarossa, who would some day come out of his cave and restore Germany to her rightful greatness.

The Germans have been telling us fairy tales for more than 100 years. Why shouldn't they continue to tell them to us if it worked during all that time?

But we are fools if we fail to understand that we can expect nothing but dreams of world conquest, and murders, and wholesale slaughter, to live on in German minds for many, many years to come. How long it will take them to shed those inborn, burning ideas, no one can predict.

It is equally unpredictable in the case of the Japanese. They too are bowing, scraping and talking to us with their hats in hand. Yet even in defeat, the Japanese arrogance continues as his dominant characteristic. It is impossible to recall one written or spoken word in which they have admitted defeat.

Jusue Oya, chief of the Overseas Bureau of the Japan Broadcasting Corporation, broke the news to the Japanese with these words:

"We have bowed to the enemy's material and scientific power. However, *in spiritual power we have not lost*. We do not think the way we have thought has been wrong. We have lost, but this is only temporary."

The way the Japs have thought included such curious thoughts as enslaving 300 million natives in Asia; using Chinese and British Empire troops as live bayonet dummies; executing American and Australian fliers for non-existent atrocities; starving, beating, murdering thousands of American, British, Australian, and Chinese civilian internees and prisoners-of-war.

Is it any wonder, with such curious thoughts predominating, the resigning Japanese cabinet exhorted the Japanese with this parting message:

"We, the Cabinet, here repress our tears of grief and dare to request our comrades *to seek this revenge.*"

We must not forget that drastic methods must continue to be imposed on the Japanese to impress on their minds irrevocably that they are a beaten, thoroughly defeated people, militarily and psychologically. For Japan this temporary military and naval reverse may very well be construed as a victory because their

Emperor (and the myth surrounding him) remains on the throne; their army, although thoroughly and effi-ciently demobilized by General MacArthur, is still intact and their manpower has not been destroyed. In some respects, the Japs bear even more watching than the Germans.

But vigilance as to both Germany and Japan must be eternal. We must never relax our guard a single moment. Our tough treatment of the enemies will not be a matter involving humanity, compassion or mercy, but something we take for granted—self-defense.

We must never be allowed to forget that even the greatest and most fertile scientific brains we possess, which gave us the atomic bomb, have not been able to invent any weapon of warfare which can shoot and kill an idea.

# XIII
# HAVE WE WON?

We have a war to win right in our own backyard—in the United States of America. If we don't fight it, or if we fight it half-heartedly and we lose, then we shall have lost the war and we shall have allowed Germany and Japan, even in unconditional surrender, to win the victory for which they planned.

This war is the fight against racial and religious prejudice which allowed German's invisible war against this country to flourish and throw us into such confusion in 1939, 1940 and 1941, we didn't know which way to turn. All of which gave Hitler and Japan more time to build up their military offensive against us.

Joseph Goebbels, the world's most successful hand at creating racial, religious and internal friction to the advantage of Nazism, once said:

"Nothing will be easier than to produce a bloody revolution in America. No other country has so many social and racial tensions. We shall be able to play on many strings here."

What is even more frightening than those words is the fact that that's exactly what Goebbels and all of Hitler's little helpers, both of the German and of the native variety, succeeded in doing in these United States while we were busy playing golf, bridge, baseball and drinking highballs.

Goebbels knew that 135,000,000 Americans were descended from 58 different national origins and adhered to 252 different religious sects. Goebbels played it for all it was worth. An Army Service Force Manual issued in October 1944, warned: "Enemy attempts to cause confusion in the United States through the spread of racial doctrines have made it particularly necessary that there be frank and objective discussions of this subject during the present war. The doctrine of Aryan superiority has become one of the dominant factors in the present world struggle. Hitler has made this doctrine 'the reason' for untold aggression and devastation. Likewise, on the other side of the world, the Japanese have been trying to demonstrate their inherent superiority."

The Japanese, who are great copyers—from electric light bulbs to just bright Fascist ideas—felt that if that magical thing called "race prejudice" worked for Hitler, why not for them? Within a week after Pearl Harbor the Japanese radio was reminding us:

"How can America be fighting for racial equality when it does not exist in America?"

Jap propagandists had a field day broadcasting to the world the details of the 1943 Detroit race riots. The Japs, oppressors of millions of Chinese, Burmese and others, began championing the Negroes of the United States. Why? Because they were attempting to divide us, split our war effort and throw us into internal confusion to keep us from uniting to win the war. The Japs knew that American Negroes comprise about one-tenth of America's population and therefore an important minority. And Hitler showed that minority problems, i.e. Sudeten Germans, Germans in Poland, etc.—can be exploited to the advantage of Fascism.

We, as Americans, have nothing to be proud of in our history of prejudice and dealing with minority groups. At one time or another we have deprived of their religious and political rights Catholics, Quakers, Jews, Lutherans, Moravians, Presbyterians, Baptists, deists and atheists.

In 1850 the "Know Nothing" Party was formed to fight Irish and Catholic immigrants. Eventually our discrimination turned against Poles, Italians, Slavs, Jews and Russians. The history of the Ku Klux Klan in the United States is one which should warm the heart of every good Nazi. The Klan doesn't like Negroes, Jews and Catholics and promotes "white supremacy," just as Hitler sponsored "aryan supremacy."

History and Hitler have taught us that the first scapegoat is not the last. After the first group, which may be Jews, Catholics or organized labor, it then becomes, Masons, Elks, Odd Fellows, Baptists and any other minority. The rise of all dictators has been over the bodies of minorities sloughed off one at a time.

It never occurs to most of us that the United States became great because it was the melting pot of all the genius, ambition, dreams, abilities and skills of the world. Refugee Jews played a leading part in giving the atom bomb to America.

Prejudice makes impossible any real solution of economic, social or personal difficulties. The Nazis proved that to us beyond any doubt. They told 65 million Germans that all social and economic ills are due to 600,000 Germans who happened to be Jews. The Nazis imprisoned, murdered or exiled all except a handful of German Jews. Instead of decreasing German troubles, it quadrupled their plight because it deprived Germany of the abilities and skills of an important minority. Today, with practically no Jews in the country, Germany's troubles as a defeated nation are greater and more numerous than ever.

The War Department continued to stress racial prejudice as an acute danger to victory when one of its pamphlets stated:

"To contribute by act or word toward the increase of misunderstanding, suspicion and tension between peoples of different racial and national origins in this country and among our Allies is to help the enemy!"

The Germans thought that racial and religious prejudice was important enough a weapon to use at the battlefronts, where the German's prime objective always was to kill as many Americans as was possible. They considered the use of racial and religious prejudice against our troops as important as firing an 88mm shell or nebelwerfers (six-barreled mortars) at them. They felt it was as important to hit our prejudices as to fire death-dealing artillery.

On the American Fifth Army front, Anti-Semitic leaflets thrown by the Germans to our soldiers were commonplace. Anti-Semitism has been part of a world crusade with the Germans, and if the Germans hadn't thought it would work against our soldiers, the Germans wouldn't have used it. These leaflets were cleverly mixed up with sex and pornography to catch our soldiers' attention.

To the 92nd Division, the first all-Negro combat infantry division, the Germans threw a stinger headed: "Is this what you're fighting for?" and then varied the leaflet with pictures; of the Detroit race riot, or the photograph of a Negro lynching, or some other photograph showing discrimination against the Negro in the United States. If the Nazis thought it as important as a weapon which killed the body, then we Americans are the world's biggest suckers if we don't take notice and learn the horrible lesson taught us by a bitter, deadly enemy.

The Germans did their work well in the field of religious and racial prejudice in the United States. One German propagandist captured in Italy, told the writer:

"It will not be necessary for us to return to America for some years to come. What we have done there will hold indefinitely."

If there is one thing which will lose us the total war, it will be our racial and religious prejudices fanned by the Nazi propaganda to which we have been exposed in one form or another for more than twelve long years.

Struthers Burt, discussing minorities, said:

"Prejudice is a wart, rub it and it grows; prejudice is a black mole, as it spreads it becomes a cancer. Prejudice is a prairie fire, a spark can make a conflagration.

"When the present king of Denmark was asked if Denmark has a Jewish problem, he smiled. 'We have no minority problems in Denmark,' he said, 'because no Dane considers himself inferior to anyone.'"

There is no magic formula to wipe out prejudice and hatred. It will surely not be done overnight or by pressing a button. It calls for a widespread better understanding and interchange of knowledge among all racial and religious groups. It could start with education and equal job opportunities for all. It may be that better housing, more political freedom or more social freedom, is the solution.

But over all hangs the urgent necessity that we had better attack the problem before it attacks and defeats us. Psychological warfare is cumulative. If it continues to build up, we are doomed.

Now, with the Germans defeated, it will be difficult to tell Americans who promote racial and religious hatred, that they're playing "Hitler's game," "Goebbel's game," or "the Nazi game." There is no comparison because the shooting is over. It is safer, as a measure of common sense self-defense to remember that the shooting is over but the war is not.

We will not have won that final victory until we wipe out completely everything which our enemy stood for. The United States is the best place to begin that process, and thus beat enemy psychological warfare at its own game. When we have no weaknesses, such as racial or religious hatreds, then only shall we be immune to psychological warfare's attacks and poisons.

President Truman in a recent message to Congress summed up the world's current task of consolidating the military and naval victory when he said:

"We have won a great war—we the united nations of plain people who hate war. In the test of that war we found a strength of unity that brought us through—a strength that crushed the power of those who sought by force to deny our faith in the dignity of man.

"During this trial the voices of disunity among us were silent or were subdued to an occasional whine that warned us that they were still among us. Those voices are beginning to cry aloud again. We must learn constantly to turn deaf ears to them. They are voices which foster fear and suspicion and intolerance and hate. They seek to destroy our harmony, our understanding of each other, our American tradition of 'live and let live.' They have become busy again, trying to set race against race, creed against creed, farmer against city dweller, worker against employer, people against their own governments. They seek only to do us mischief. They must not prevail. . . ."

# XIV
# PROPAGANDA AND THE PEACE

America was not playing at the game of psychological warfare for keeps. It was all a temporary bit of business which, like the business of shooting and killing the enemy, just had to be done. This was most unfortunate because America, except as represented by the American soldier, is unknown to the world.

America is still a far-away myth to most peoples of the world. Even to the people of Great Britain, who should know America well because of a common language and common traditions, the United States is a series of contradictions, misunderstandings and puzzles.

When this writer was in Italy during the war, he found a remarkable ignorance about America and Americans. Even the most intelligent Italians saw America only through the eyes of American movies—obviously of the grade 'Z' variety—from newspaper reports of Hollywood divorces, Chicago gang murders, violence during labor disputes, and the more-than-ordinary-run of American screwballiana. One Italian solemnly said: "You Americans are all immoral. You divorce."

The same ignorance about America was evident in all the other countries visited—in Greece, North Africa, France, Belgium, Austria, Switzerland and Denmark. At the same time, there was a great hunger for facts about America and Americans.

This need is not being met except in a small way. The U. S. Office of War Information and its State Department successor have had budget trouble. It seems that Congress is convinced that the more ignorance there is of America in the rest of the world, the less trouble America will have in the future.

An Italian politician of the fascist stripe told the writer: "If we had known that America's sympathy was with Britain, we never would have entered the war on the side of Germany."

The same was heard from a score of other Italians in a position to know the real mood of the Italian people before "the stab in the back" of June 10, 1940. It is not too much to say that if Italy had stayed out of the war, there would be at least 20,000 more American soldiers alive today.

During the war, American propaganda stressed America's huge production capacity and the inevitability of an Allied victory. At the same time, emphasis was also placed on the certain defeat of Germany and Japan. But at no time did we try to sell either the enemy, our allies or neutrals on the advantages of America's form of democracy. This was a great mistake.

It would not have been a question of ramming America down the throat of a Slovene; it would have been good insurance to give him a clear picture of what America stood for—other than winning the war and liberating those enslaved by the Germans.

Francis Williams, the British publicist, states in his recent book, *Press, Parliament and People:* "Because public opinion is now, and very properly, so large a factor in foreign policy, it is important that every means should be used to inform the ordinary citizen of the facts upon which sensible judgment can be formed and without which it cannot."

American public opinion, no matter how some writers disdain it, is the most powerful in the world. Besides having industrial, military and naval might to back it, American public opinion is the most free of any in the world; and, by the same token, swings the greatest weight among the peoples of the world—even among the blustering, tough-talking Russians.

American public opinion reaches the world principally through the competitive news agencies of the world; three of them—Associated Press, United Press and International News Service—American-owned and operated. By the very necessity of speed and competition, the news services frequently convey only a "sensationalist" view of America. Cable tolls far from favorable to American press associations (especially in British spheres of influence) are another factor which cut down wordage and consequently reduce understanding of America to a mere surface scratching.

Who, then, can tell America's story?

The United States of America has come-of-age in the world of international affairs, although some segments of the American people are not quite ready to accept the responsibility. In its coming-of-age, it is America's duty to tell its own story to the world.

Free interchange of news and information is properly the job of free press associations. They should continue the job with a deep sense of responsibility: what they transmit will affect the feelings of peoples everywhere, toward America and toward democracy. But, by their very limitations, the press associations cannot do the job completely.

We are very well aware that the right words properly put together, delivered at the right spot at the right moment, can capture and kill. Why not use words and ideas as an instrument of peace, rather than as an instrument of death?

A longing for peace is deep in the hearts of all decent peoples everywhere. There are good arguments for those who insist that the best way to maintain the peace is to maintain a war machine to police the world and to keep the peace by force.

Why not, then, the establishment of a U.S. Department of Information on the same status as the War Department and the Navy Department? Why not a U.S. Department of Information to police the world with words of truth?

COACHWHIP PUBLICATIONS

COACHWHIPBOOKS.COM

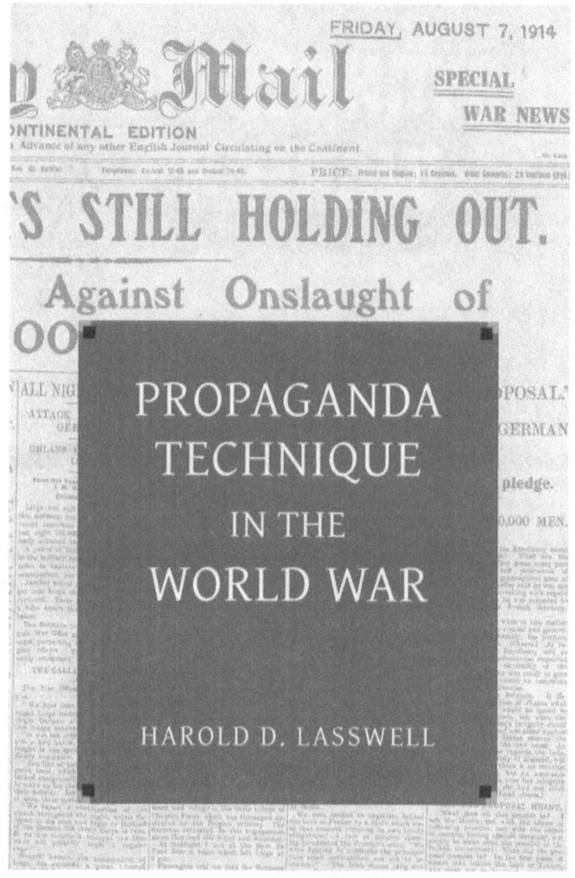
FRIDAY, AUGUST 7, 1914
SPECIAL
WAR NEWS
STILL HOLDING OUT.
Against Onslaught of
PROPAGANDA
TECHNIQUE
IN THE
WORLD WAR
HAROLD D. LASSWELL

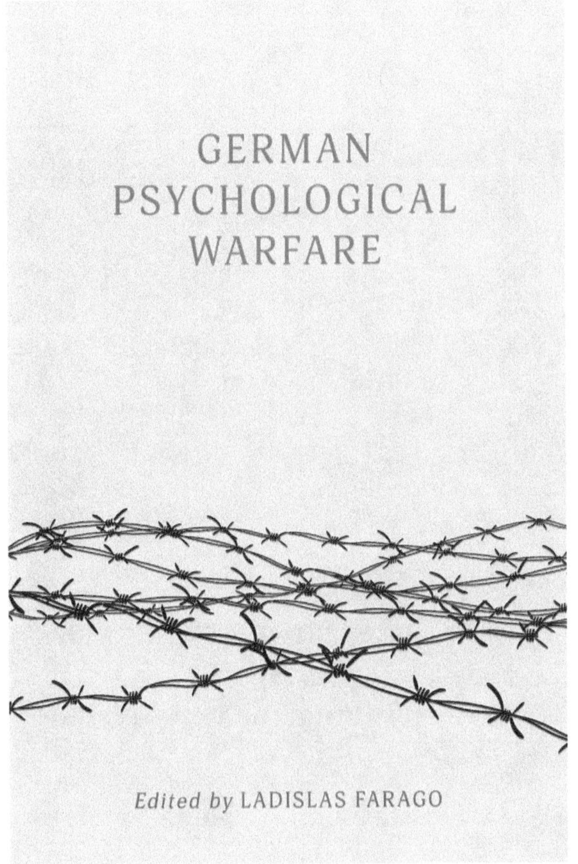
GERMAN
PSYCHOLOGICAL
WARFARE
Edited by LADISLAS FARAGO

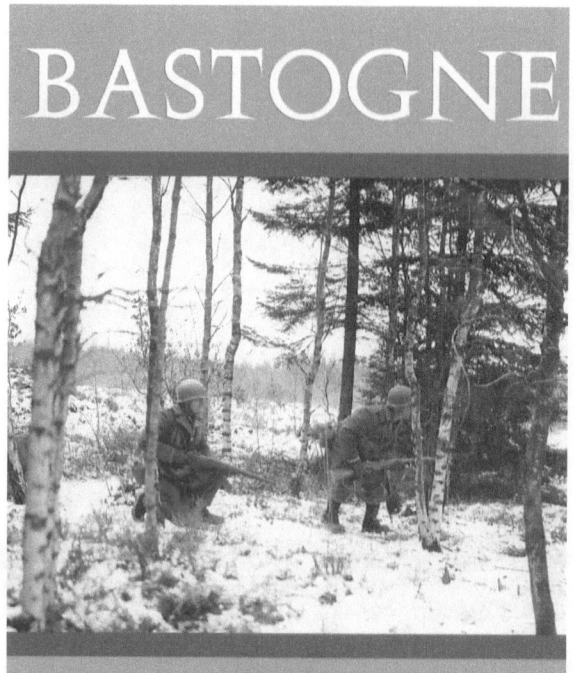

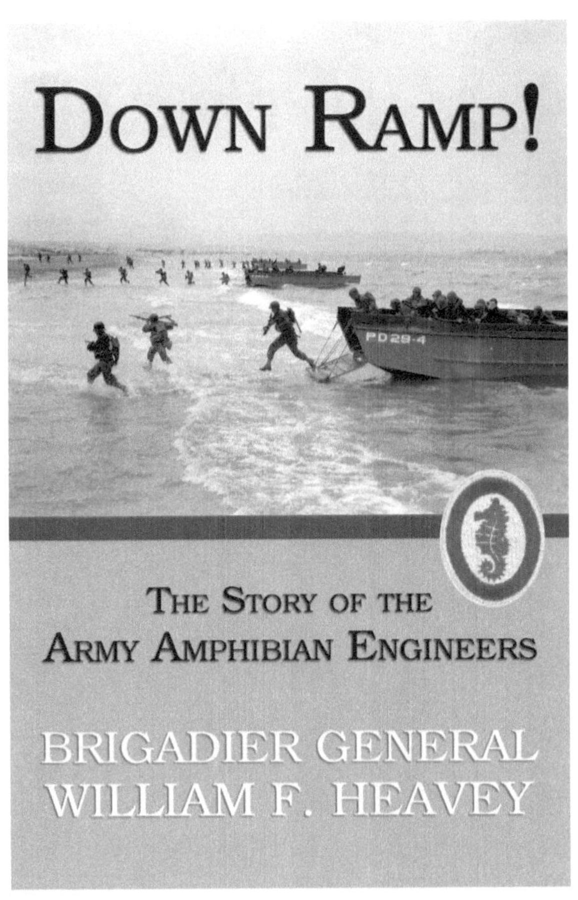
DOWN RAMP!
PD 28-4
THE STORY OF THE
ARMY AMPHIBIAN ENGINEERS
BRIGADIER GENERAL
WILLIAM F. HEAVEY

HANDBOOK
FOR SPIES
ALEXANDER FOOTE

COACHWHIP PUBLICATIONS

COACHWHIPBOOKS.COM

www.ingramcontent.com/pod-product-compliance
Lightning Source LLC
Chambersburg PA
CBHW030506260626
47157CB00005B/1678

* 9 7 8 1 6 1 6 4 6 4 9 2 9 *